C000299704

CONTENTS

INTRODUCTION

This booklet has been compiled by members of the History Group of the Holywood District University of the Third Age (U3A).

After careful consideration we have selected for inclusion around 70 individuals and families, past and present, associated with the town of Holywood and the surrounding district. Most have lived here, some have also worked here, while a few have more tenuous connections with Holywood, but were nevertheless deemed worthy of inclusion.

There can be no quantitative criteria; we have sought to assess the significance of the individual's contribution to the development of Holywood or wider society, and which may have resonance today. The majority of our entries are deceased – it is naturally easier to assess an individual's 'worth' after the end of their life.

We are very conscious that no arbitrary selection of this kind will please everyone; indeed many readers will wish to advance the cause of their own choices. We welcome that, in part as a way of stimulating further research and debate. (It should also be noted that a few individuals declined our invitation to feature.)

This exercise reminds us both of the cultural richness of our town, and the impact that its residents have had on the wider community. While some have travelled widely in their chosen occupations and callings, many have retained their roots in Holywood.

We have tried to achieve a broad spectrum in our selection, in terms of class, creed and gender.

We have grouped the entries by areas of interest, eg arts or business, as a way of bringing together like-minded individuals. Again this approach is inevitably somewhat arbitrary. (We do appreciate that many of the individuals could be listed under more than one heading, so varied have been their interests and contributions.) Within each category, we have used alphabetical order.

And there are some individuals whom we have grouped together on the page, in a way that we trust makes sense for the reader. There are others about whom it may be thought their merits cannot adequately be described in around 400 words, but we have accepted that discipline in our drafting.

We have sought, wherever possible, to include either one image of the person, or an illustration associated with them – preferably both. The exercise has reminded us of how much of their work and memorials can still be seen in Holywood today.

The members of the Holywood District U3A History Group would like to express their sincere thanks to a considerable number of people and sources without whom this work would not have been possible, including the splendid staff at Holywood Library, friends and colleagues who have helped with research or in drafting individual articles, and relatives of the selected individuals who have kindly viewed text prior to publication.

Additional information about the historical figures and their dwellings in Holywood can be found in Con Auld's book *Holywood Co. Down, Then and Now* (published in 2002), and Tony Merrick's book *Buildings of Holywood* (published in 1986).

Finally, while we have done our best to be as accurate as possible, we apologise in advance for any errors or omissions. We trust too that if we have unwittingly failed to acknowledge the source of material or images correctly, this will be pardoned.

We are most grateful to the Belfast City Airport for a grant toward the cost of publication.

All the profits from sales of the book will go to charity.

This book has been compiled by Grace Burnside, Pat Clarke, Valerie Cobain, Norma Cooper, Audrey Lockhart, Betty McLaughlin, Robin Masefield, and Joan Whiteside.

SECTION ONE – THE ARTS

E GODFREY BROWN

Godfrey Brown was an Englishman to whom the town of Holywood and the city of Belfast can be very grateful.

Born in Barrow-in-Furness in 1874, Godfrey Brown came to Northern Ireland in 1912 as Conductor of the Belfast Philharmonic Society, holding the post for the next 38 years. It was the beginning of an era, as he had a unique place in the musical life of Ulster.

The position of organist and choirmaster of Holywood parish church came available at the same time and Godfrey Brown was successful in securing it, so he and his wife settled in Holywood at *Fernbank* at the top of Downshire Road. He loved the parish church and was loved and admired in return by those he taught.

In 1924, Brown was appointed Director of Music at the newly-established BBC station in Belfast. Much of its output then was music. He was awarded the OBE in 1936.

He also conceived the idea of a Music Festival in Holywood and, as chairman, had to overcome great difficulties, not least when the Town Hall – the venue chosen, was burnt down in the 1940s; the resourcefulness of Godfrey Brown suggested Grainger Bros. contractors' shed! Being in close proximity to the railway station led to some unscheduled minor intervals – when a train was due at the same time as a performer was on stage, the adjudicator would ring his bell, and indicate that the performance had better be delayed for a few minutes. This was all just part of the pattern, and was accepted with amused good humour!

The first Music Festival was held in 1948 and is still in existence 70 years later, the venue for many years being the Queen's Hall – not just so close to the railway station! Godfrey Brown remained Director until his death on 2 February 1955.

At his funeral service in Holywood parish church, the Vicar of Holywood, Reverend Eric Barber paid tribute to his organist and choirmaster: '*Godfrey Brown was a great man; his vast musical knowledge, his impeccable taste, his concentration on detail, his hatred of anything careless or slipshod, made his concerts to be looked forward to and remembered.*'

The blue plaque on his former house in Downshire Road

Godfrey Brown is buried in Redburn Cemetery. A blue plaque can be seen at his former home *Fernbank* in recognition of this gentleman who gave so much to the town of Holywood – '*E. Godfrey Brown 1874-1955, Musician*'. In 2018, a commemorative plaque was re-erected in the Queen's Hall.

COLIN DAVIDSON

Colin Davidson is an Irish visual artist, living and working not far from Holywood. An artist who works in themes, his recent large-scale head paintings have been exhibited worldwide.

Davidson was born in Belfast in 1968 and attended Methodist College, Belfast between 1980 and 1987. He graduated from the University of Ulster in 1991 with a First Class Honours Degree in Design. He worked in the field of design for print until 1999 when he started to paint full-time. Davidson is an Academician of the Royal Ulster Academy and served as President of the Royal Ulster Academy between 2012 and 2015.

Davidson started to paint Belfast in his teens, and this theme came to the fore in 2004 when his exhibition *No Continuing City* was mounted at the Tom Caldwell Gallery. The exhibition included large paintings of Belfast as seen from high view-points. The urban theme continued between 2006 and 2010 when Davidson made paintings based on the illusionary world seen in city window reflections.

Since 2010 Davidson's work has been concerned with the human face and the resulting large scale head paintings are now recognised internationally. His portraits of Brad Pitt, Seamus Heaney and Michael Longley are held in the collection of the Smithsonian National

Colin Davidson in front of his painting

Portrait Gallery in Washington DC, the Ulster Museum in Belfast, and the National Gallery of Ireland in Dublin respectively.

A permanent exhibition of Davidson's work is on display at the Lyric Theatre in Belfast, where he presented his work to Her Majesty Queen Elizabeth II and the President of Ireland during the Royal visit to Northern Ireland in 2012.

Davidson's work has been exhibited in the BP Portrait Award at the National Portrait Gallery in London in 2011, 2012 and 2013. In 2012 he won the Visitors' Choice Award.

In 2015, in an exhibition at the Ulster Museum entitled *Silent Testimony*, Davidson unveiled 18 very evocative new paintings exploring the suffering and loss caused to ordinary people by the Troubles in Northern Ireland. In December 2015 he was commissioned by *Time* Magazine to paint the German Chancellor, Angela Merkel, for the cover for its *Person of the Year* issue.

In 2016, he was commissioned to paint a portrait of Queen Elizabeth II for Co-operation Ireland. This painting was unveiled at Crosby Hall in London by the Queen in November 2016.

JOHN T DAVIS

John T Davis is Northern Ireland's most distinctive documentary film-maker and cinematographer. Born in Holywood, in 1947, he showed an early talent for technical design and from 1967 to 1971 studied painting at Belfast College of Art.

The death in 1974 of his maternal uncle, John "Jack" McBride Neill, the architect of Bangor's famous *Tonic* Cinema, had a profound effect on his subsequent career. As well as inheriting from his uncle *Ben Edar*, the historic house on the shore of Belfast Lough at Marino, he also acquired an old 8mm film camera which enabled John to make his first film, *Transfer* (1975).

John began his professional film-making career in 1977 as cameraman and director on a range of industrial films. His personal vision and poetic style characterise the many feature documentary films he has directed. These include *Shellshock Rock* (1979), a radical record of Northern Ireland's punk scene, his epic road film *Route 66* (1985), which explored the music and attitudes of middle America along the famous highway, and *Dust on the Bible* and *Power in the Blood* (1989).

John T Davis with his uncle's old projector

Heart on the Line (1990) looked at the songwriters of Nashville, while *Hobo* (1991) required Davis to spend three months living as a hobo, with a concealed camera, jumping freight trains. He then directed *Hip to the Tip: Atlantic – The Independent Years* (1993), *Van Morrison Live in Santa Monica* (1994) and *The Uncle Jack* (1996).

Tragically, on a stormy night in December 1999, his house *Ben Edar* was seriously damaged by fire. Much of his archive, including many irreplaceable films and photographic records, was lost. He has since made several more films, among them *Traveller* (2000), *A House Divided* (2003), and *Tailwind* (2008). John's films have been screened at festivals and symposia round the world, and he has received many awards. He was elected to the prestigious Aosdana in 2005 for his contribution to the arts in Ireland.

Music is a prominent feature in John's films, and he has become an accomplished lyricist and performer of his unique brand of Western Country music.

The confluence between John's film-making and song-writing is evident in lyrics and melodies sourced in affinity with the people, places and musical styles of North America. His songs build on the ballad tradition of America's working cowboys, and the romanticism of Hollywood's singing cowboys. John has recorded two CDs entitled *Last Western Cowboy* and *Indigo Snow*.

JAMIE DORNAN

Jamie Dornan was born on 1 May 1982, in Belfast and grew up in Holywood. He has two older sisters, Liesa who works for Universal in London, and Jessica who is the founder of a tech start-up (Afterbook) and based in Northern Ireland. His father Jim Dornan is a well-known obstetrician and gynaecologist, who also considered becoming an actor in his youth. (Jamie is also related to Greer Garson.) When Jamie was 16 his mother, Lorna, died from cancer.

Jamie went to Methodist College, Belfast where he played rugby and took part in the drama department. He later attended Teesside University, leaving to participate in the Channel 4 television show, *Model Behaviour*, where he was encouraged to move to London full time. There he began his modelling and acting career.

He performed with the folk band 'Sons of Jim' until it disbanded in 2008. They were the support group for the Scottish songwriter K T Tunstall on tour. Jamie was also a popular model, working for Abercrombie & Fitch and later for Aquascutum, Hugo Boss and Armani. He did major ad campaigns with Dior Homme and Calvin Klein (with Kate Moss and Eva Mendes) and was labelled 'The Golden Torso' by the New York Times.

His first film role was as Axel von Fersen in Sofia Coppola's *Marie Antoinette* in 2006. More recently he was known for his portrayal of Christian Grey in *Fifty Shades of Grey* released in 2014 and the follow up films in 2017 and 2018. He also appeared as Jan Kubis in *Anthropoid*.

On television, he played Sheriff Graham Humbert in the ABC Series *Once Upon A Time* (2011-2013). He then starred alongside Gillian Anderson in the Northern Ireland Drama series (2013-16), shown on BBC and RTE, *The Fall*, playing a serial killer terrorising Belfast. He was nominated for a British Academy Television Award for Best Actor and won the IFTA for Best Actor.

People's Magazine readers have voted him the third sexiest man alive and on similar lists in other magazines his name always appears.

In 2010 Jamie met English singer-song writer Amelia Warner and they married in 2013. They have two daughters, and live in England. Jamie is a huge sports fan – namely rugby, golf and football. He often attends and participates in pro-am golf tournaments.

GARTH ENNIS

Garth Ennis, a comic book writer, was born in Holywood in 1970, the son of Tom and Evie Ennis. He attended Sullivan Upper School. His work is known for graphic violence, satire and black comedy, but at his best he writes with humanity and fearlessness.

He began his writing career in 1989 with the series *Troubled Souls* followed by *For a Few Troubles More*, both set in Northern Ireland. These appeared in the short-lived but well received British Anthology, *Crisis*.

Some of the most notable works in which he has been involved are *Preacher, The Boys, Judge Dredd, Hell Blazer, Punisher, Dan Dare, Just a Pilgrim* and *Hitman*.

His work has been illustrated by artists such as the late Steve Dillon, Glenn Fabry, John McCrea and Carlos Esquerra. He has written for *Crisis* parent publication *2000 AD*, and the American Publishers DC Comics, Vertigo, Valiant, Marvel, Avatar, and Virgin etc.

These works have won him many accolades in the Comic Book field including three Will Eisner awards in 1998 and 1999 for "Best Writer", "Best Single Issue" and a "Best Continuing Series" award for *Preacher*. Numerous others include four UK Comic Art Awards.

Preacher has since been adapted to produce the Drama/Fantasy Television series *Preacher*. In 2011 he wrote and directed a short film *Stitched* and elements from his story *Dangerous Habits* were used in the film *Constantine*.

He is not a fan of the American superhero genre of comics, and has produced work in which the whole world of superheroes is parodied in a very unflattering and subversive manner.

His interest in comics has led him to research widely on both the First and Second World Wars and he has written many graphic novels, using war as his theme. Most are written from the point of view of the ordinary soldier, airman or airwoman and the civilians caught up in the mindless horror and pointlessness of it all.

Garth and his wife Ruth are American citizens who live in New York.

ROWEL FRIERS

Rowel Friers was born in Belfast on 13 April 1920 – the year of partition in Ireland – and he died on 21 September 1998, in the wake of the Belfast Agreement that April.

He was first employed as an apprentice lithographer but after four years he went to study full-time at the Belfast College of Art from 1935 to 1942. He began publishing his cartoons in the 1940s and his work appeared in *Punch,* the *Radio Times, London Opinion,* the *Daily Express,* the *Sunday Independent, Dublin Opinion,* the *Northern Whig,* the *Newsletter,* the *Irish Times* and the *Belfast Telegraph.* He also became a leading figure in the Ulster Watercolour Society and was President of the Royal Ulster Academy of Arts from 1993 to 1997.

The May Queen

But in the 1960s, when the political situation in Northern Ireland began to deteriorate, Friers felt compelled to provide ongoing comment on the 'politics of the day' through his cartoons, which were published in the local newspapers. The journalist Billy Simpson wrote: '*He understands the Ulsterman as no sociologist ever will. And he has the gift of portraying that understanding in art and words that enable us to laugh at ourselves'.*

Friers' work displays affection for the people of Northern Ireland even while he vented his frustration at their political leaders. His humour was subtle but incisive. Conor O'Brien said '*He is …a pin-pricker of inflated egos!*' The poet, Michael Longley said '*In Rowel Friers we have … an embodiment of the kind of future we need.'*

Rowel and his wife, Yvonne, were a great team as she enjoyed drama and he enjoyed designing the stage sets – first for Fisherwick Dramatic Society and then for Holywood Players. Together with a friend, Yvonne ran a playgroup in 'unused space' in the Friers family home on the corner of Brook Street and Victoria Road for over 30 years.

Rowel and Yvonne's grandson is young Rowel, a prodigy pianist studying at the Royal Irish Academy of Music and who was awarded aged 14, a distinction in the Diploma Associate Trinity College, London (equivalent to a university undergraduate degree and the highest mark ever awarded in Northern Ireland). In 2017 Rowel was invited to perform in Carnegie Hall, New York.

GEORGE FREDERICK MORRIS HARDING

Morris Harding was born in Hertfordshire in April 1874. After a stint in the Merchant Navy, he trained as a painter and sculptor in the studio of his uncle, Harry Bates (who was a leading figure in the New Sculpture movement). Harding also taught sculpture at the London County Council Technical Institute. His work was exhibited at the Royal Academy in London and the Glasgow Institute.

One of Harding's first major commissions was a series of relief panels at London Zoo, depicting polar bears, a subject to which he returned on a number of occasions. He also worked on a number of important war memorials on which animals featured and he was commissioned to execute a major work for the Memorial Chapel at Rugby School in 1922. The architect of this project was Sir Charles Nicholson who became a consultant to the Cathedral Church of St Anne, Belfast at a crucial stage in its construction.

Painting of his house on Church Road by Joanna Martin

In 1925, Harding was invited by Nicholson to work on his designs for many of the capitals and corbels in the nave of St Anne's. Along with other carvings and the bronze soldier on top of the memorial lectern to the fallen of the 36th (Ulster) Division, this body of work became the major undertaking of his career, and occupied his creative talents for much of the next 23 years. It could be said that his contribution to the ornamentation of St Anne's represented a labour of love. During the Blitz, he volunteered to keep overnight fire watch in the Cathedral when the city was under threat of attack.

Other commissions in Northern Ireland followed – the font in St Peter's Church, Antrim Road, and the Royal Arms on Telephone House, Cromac Street in Belfast and those on Hillsborough Castle. He also carved the tomb of the 7th Marquess of Londonderry, in the grounds of Mountstewart.

Harding shared Rosamond Praeger's studio in Holywood for a time, carving the base for her landmark sculpture – *Johnny the Jig*. He eventually settled in Holywood, with his own studio in Church Road. He became President of the Royal Ulster Academy in 1947, was awarded the OBE in 1950, and an Honorary Master of Arts degree from Queen's University in 1958. He died at his home in January 1964.

His considerable contribution to our built heritage has been largely forgotten, and his remains lie in an unmarked grave in Holywood's New Cemetery. A blue plaque at his former home (in Church Hill Terrace) celebrates his contribution.

FRANK McKELVEY

Frank McKelvey was born in Belfast on 3 June 1895.

His father was a painter and interior decorator. The young Frank worked as a lithographer and poster designer before entering the Belfast School of Art. He won the *Sir Charles Brett* prize for figure drawing there in 1912. One of his works from that year is a charming pen and ink drawing of a friend and fellow student.

By 1918 his work was exhibited at the Royal Hibernian Academy in Dublin and in 1921 he was elected a member of the Belfast Art Society. McKelvey was appointed an associate of the RHA in 1923, being granted full membership in 1930.

McKelvey's best known works are landscapes of Irish scenery. During his career McKelvey was considered on a par with Paul Henry and James Humbert Craig, two of the most successful Irish landscape painters of the time. One of his most important commissions was to paint pictures of 'Old Belfast', which collection is in the Ulster Museum.

But he was also an accomplished portrait painter and was represented in the *Irish Portraits by Ulster Artists* exhibition. He painted many of his contemporaries in various spheres of Ulster life – academicians, clerics and businessmen. Many were commissioned and went straight to private homes or to Boardrooms, so his landscapes were better known to the wider public. Examples of his work are on display in many municipal galleries across Ireland, as well as in the Ulster Museum.

A pen and ink drawing done of a fellow student when Frank was at Art College

McKelvey was elected as one of the first academicians of the Ulster Academy of Arts when it was founded in 1930.

In 1936, Dutch people living in Ireland presented three landscapes by McKelvey to Princess Juliana as a wedding present.

McKelvey lived on My Lady's Mile in Holywood for a period, in his later years. He died on 30 June 1974.

SOPHIA ROSAMOND PRAEGER

Rosamond Praeger is probably Northern Ireland's leading sculptor. She was the only daughter of six children of linen merchant William Praeger and his wife Maria (née Patterson). She was born on 15 April 1867, just before the family moved from the Crescent to *Woodburn House* on Croft Road, Holywood.

Rosamond in her studio

Her education began at Rev McAlester's school underneath Holywood's Non-Subscribing Presbyterian church, before she moved to Sullivan Upper School in 1879. At just 15, she enrolled at the School of Art in Belfast. Two years later she went to the Slade School of Art in London, where she studied under Alphonse Legros who influenced her development as an artist and sculptress. After winning prizes for drawing and modelling in clay, she lived briefly in Paris before returning to Holywood.

Initially she illustrated others' books, and then her own children's books. She also wrote poetry and had an interest in Celtic folklore. She became a keen member of the Belfast Naturalists' Field Club. Before long she turned her hand to sculpture, with a studio in Belfast. (She had become interested in working in stone through Holywood stonemason, John Lowry.) The commercial success of her sculpture *The Philosopher* enabled her in 1914 to build a studio in Hibernia Street in Holywood (*St Brigid's*, which she shared with fellow sculptor Morris Harding). The site is identified with a blue plaque.

Rosamond is known for the bronze sculpture of *Johnny the Jig*; the original is on display in North Down Museum. It commemorates Fergus Morton, a young Boy Scout, tragically killed at Easter 1952.

Other works included church memorials (some after the Great War), plaster casts and bronzes (eg the *Waif* in Holywood Library, where there is also a display of several works). She produced a wide range of plaques, figures and busts, some exhibited in Belfast or Dublin. She also left many sketches, and painted landscapes in watercolours.

She and her mother had moved to *Derryquin* on the Old Cultra Road in 1891. In 1902, Rosamond was elected a vice-president of the Royal Ulster Academy of Arts. In 1939, she was awarded the MBE, and a year later Queen's University gave her an honorary degree. She died on 16 April 1954, at *Rock Cottage*, Cultra. She is commemorated on the headstone in the Old Priory Graveyard, which she designed for her father, and through her bequest of Praeger's Field as a recreation area – on the Coastal path from the town towards Seapark.

In 2006 Con Auld published *Rosamond Praeger, The Way That She Went*; Dr Joseph McBrinn has also written *Sophia Rosamond Praeger 1867-1954, Art, Literature, Science,* (2014).

BRIAN AND LISA BALLARD

Brian Ballard is a well-known local artist. Born in Belfast in 1943, he first trained at the Belfast College of Art before continuing at the Liverpool College of Art. He then worked in the 1960s for the Arts Council of Northern Ireland.

Although now living in Belfast, the artist lived for some time in Holywood where his daughter Lisa and sons Marc and Ross grew up. He also spends long periods on the picturesque island of Inishfree Upper, off the coast of Donegal.

Four books, painted by Brian Ballard

Choosing to paint mainly simple scenes of still life or landscapes, Ballard was inspired by his response to everyday objects such as a vase of flowers, an iron or a figure. Perhaps the most striking feature of Ballard's work is his intense use of colour which vibrantly illuminates the canvas. Decisive brushstrokes in strong, contrasting hues dominate the canvas. Through his technical abilities with both the paintbrush and palette knife, the artist creates energy within the composition by portraying multiple textures throughout.

He was elected into the Royal Ulster Academy of Arts. Examples of his work can be found in the collections of the Arts Councils of Ireland and Northern Ireland, and the Ulster Museum.

Lisa Ballard is a young artist who is rapidly making a name for herself. She was born in 1981, when her family were in Holywood. She attended Strathearn Grammar School and graduated in 2003 from the University of Ulster with a BA in Fine Art.

Mint wall cacti by Lisa Ballard

Lisa Ballard uses landscape to explore her obsession with colour and light, often leaning towards abstraction. Using painterly brush marks, Lisa looks beyond the landscape itself creating powerful images that reflect the temporal and fleeting nature of her experience in that place.

Lisa Ballard has already won a number of awards for her artistic flair. In 2003 at the Royal Ulster Academy Exhibition, Lisa won the *President's Prize*. Three years later again at the Royal Ulster Academy, she took home the *Original Vision* prize which was sponsored by Robinson and McIlwaine. In 2007 she was awarded the Killarney Art Gallery prize for *Young Artist under 35* at the RUA Exhibition.

Lisa Ballard's work is highly sought after by gallery owners, art dealers and private collectors throughout these islands and beyond. In 2017 she was made an Associate member of the Royal Ulster Academy.

TOM KERR AND MARK SHIELDS

Tom Kerr was born in Holywood and educated at Sullivan Upper School. He is a retired Associate of the Royal Institute of British Architects.

He took up painting in watercolours as a hobby in the 1960s and has exhibited at the Royal Ulster Academy. A very popular local artist, he has exhibited widely at home and abroad including exhibitions in Canada and New Zealand. His work is in private collections in several countries such as Germany, Holland and Australia. He now works mostly in acrylics.

He is also the author of five books of poems illustrated with his own paintings. Two of his poems from *The Quiet Shore* were chosen for inclusion in a Re-Imaging Community Project.

In 1978 he formed the Kerr Art Group which was an inspiration to many local artists. During its thirty years existence it held annual exhibitions in Holywood raising over £80,000 for charity. In 2009 Tom received an MBE for services to the Arts.

Mamore Gap by Tom Kerr

Mark Shields was born in 1963 in Northern Ireland, where he still lives. Mark was educated at Regent House School, Newtownards, and studied at the University of Ulster where he obtained a BA in Fine Art and a PGCE in Art and Design.

Developing a powerful realist style that owes much to the Old Masters, he scored early success with meticulous portraits and still-life paintings. Ambition and self-questioning have led him on to develop new ways of painting and drawing, from mysterious, atmospheric landscapes and complex narrative pictures to large-scale pastel drawings on canvas and more open abstract forms.

Shields' work has often been centred on the human figure but he continually experiments with materials and subjects in an effort to insure against falling into rhythms of working that can lead inexorably to unthinking habit.

Mark has exhibited at the Royal Academy, the National Portrait Gallery, the Royal Hibernian Academy and the Royal Ulster Academy. The artist has received various prestigious awards and portrait commissions, including H.R.H. The Prince of Wales for the Headquarters of the Royal Gurkha Rifles. In 1998 Mark was commissioned to paint the double portrait of Mary and Nicholas Robinson, which was unveiled at the National Gallery by the Taoiseach Bertie Ahern.

JOHN VINYCOMB, OLIVE HENRY AND JOHN TURNER

John Vinycomb was born in Newcastle-on-Tyne in 1833, coming to Belfast in 1855. He joined Marcus Ward and Company as an engraver where he stayed until the firm's break-up in 1899. He lived at *The Scriptorium*, Riverside, Church Road, Holywood, in the early years of the 20th century.

He was a talented artist, designer and illuminator, and also an international authority on heraldry, publishing several books eg *Fictitious and symbolic creatures in Art*. Vinycomb was President of the Belfast Ramblers' Sketching Club which developed into the Royal Ulster Academy of Arts. He also served as President of Belfast Naturalists' Field Club. Belfast City Hall has an example of his work, as have the Belfast Harbour Office and the Victoria and Albert Museum.

An Olive Henry design in First Holywood Presbyterian church.

Olive Henry is of note not only for her painting but also photography and stained glass. She was Ulster's best-known female stained glass artist. Born in Belfast in 1902, after taking evening classes at the Belfast School of Art, she was apprenticed to the Belfast glass company WF Clokey & Co. where she worked for over 50 years.

Her paintings were exhibited at the Oireachtas, the Royal Ulster Academy, the Watercolour Society of Ireland and the National Society in London.

Following the bombing of the Ulster Hospital for Women and Children in the Blitz in 1941, the Ulster Academy published a portfolio of Henry's lithographs to raise funds. She was a founding member of the Ulster Society of Women Artists, and President of the Society from 1979 to 1981. She lived latterly in Kensington Villas on Farmhill Road, and died in 1989. Her work can be seen in Holywood Presbyterian Churches and Sullivan Upper School.

John Turner was born in Belfast in 1916, training first in the Belfast College of Art before winning a scholarship to the Slade School of Art in London, then moving to Ruskin College, Oxford. In 1941 he returned; he taught art at schools in Coleraine and Downpatrick, and later at the Belfast College of Art. He was now making a reputation as a portraitist, subjects including Belfast Lord Mayors.

Turner's work often shows his pointilliste manner. 1948 saw Turner's first solo show, an *Exhibition of Portraits*, in Belfast. In 1975 he was elected a full member of the Royal Ulster Academy. When he was once asked at the RUA how to paint, he replied '*You paint what you see*'. He lived in Birch Drive and then on My Lady's Mile before his death in 2006.

HENRY CAMPBELL

Portrait of Henry Campbell,
*by kind permission of
Campbell College*

Henry Campbell was born in Newtownards in 1813. His father, who was a draper, died when Henry was one year old.

His mother's brother, Michael Campbell, owned land and a mill between Comber and Newtownards. Michael's grandson John was like a brother to Henry and featured prominently in his business life. These two boys were apprenticed to James Boomer & Co on the Falls Road where the family had a business interest. There they learned the linen trade on the shop floor.

Then Henry went to Liverpool to work in the commission trade and learn the wider business side of the industry. He returned to Belfast in 1839 aged 26, when he bought a house in Howard Street. He never married and lived with his mother. In the 1840s Henry and his cousin John acquired the flax and tow manufacturing company, Gunning and Campbell in North Howard Street, and John became the managing director.

In 1859 Henry and John bought the substantial property at Mossley from the Grimshaw family and renamed it Henry Campbell & Co. The mill was restored to profit producing raw materials for Ulster's thriving linen industry. John was the manager of the mill, while Henry as senior partner dealt with the wider business community. They pursued the philanthropic model of Victorian socialism, building a village with a school and leisure facilities for their workforce.

In the early 1870s the mill was so successful that John was able to buy Henry's share of the business and Henry retired to live in Craigavad. He bought 19 acres of land from Sir Robert Kennedy and built his grand Scottish baronial mansion which he called *Lorne*. This unassuming businessman was finally telling the world of his success. His ancestors probably came from Scotland so he marked his connection with the Campbell clan with the name of his house and the boar's head on the fireplace in his snooker room.

Henry was staunchly conservative but took no part in political life. He was a great benefactor to May Street Presbyterian Church where he worshipped, and also contributed to the foundation of Presbyterian Theological College in Belfast.

Henry died in 1889. In his will he left £280,000 (an amazing amount for a draper's son). After charitable donations and annuities and generous legacies to his nephews and nieces, there was over £200,000 left with instructions to his trustees to build a hospital or school to bear his name. Campbell College in East Belfast opened in 1894 and is still educating boys today.

JOHN CROSSLÉ

Born in Scotland in 1931, **John Crosslé** came to live in County Tyrone when he was six months old. He was first introduced to Holywood at the age of nine, when he became a boarder at Rockport Preparatory School until he was 13. During his final school years at St Columba's College, County Wicklow, he became keen on motorcycles, a passion which developed further while at Greenmount Agricultural College in Antrim.

Throughout the 1950s John worked on his father's farm in County Down, concentrating on mechanical repairs. During this time he successfully competed in motorcycle grass track racing and trials, however in 1957 he turned to four wheels and built his first racing car. The success of his 1172cc Crosslé Fords attracted purchasers at the end of each season, and a business was born.

In 1960 John and his wife Rosemary bought *Rory's Wood*, former laundry for the Dunville estate, situated at the edge of *Redburn House* grounds. Here the company rapidly expanded due to John's attention to detail and value for money ideals, coupled with innovative design and sensible construction. John continued to win many championships, but his racing career took a back seat to enable him to concentrate on car production.

In America and Europe major championship wins led to over 100 cars being produced annually during the late 1970s, with exports accounting for 80% of the company's business. Crosslé and Formula Ford were synonymous for decades, but the company also enjoyed success with its Formula 2 cars and its very popular sports racing cars.

In its sixty year history the Crosslé Car Company has produced over 1,000 cars and provided 70 jobs. With great encouragement from John, several employees utilised skills

One of the iconic Crosslé cars

learned at the factory by establishing their own companies, either in race car preparation or general engineering.

The Crosslé Car Company is the world's longest-surviving constructor of customer racing cars. Its cars have been raced world-wide, playing a significant role in the early careers of Formula One drivers including John Watson, Eddie Jordan, Eddie Irvine and Nigel Mansell. As the premises are away from public view, the hugely successful story of the Crosslé Car Company might be considered one of Holywood's best-kept secrets.

John was awarded the MBE. He and Rosemary retired in 1997, handing the business over to one of its keen customers, Arnie Black, who then ran it for 15 years. Enthusiast Paul McMorran currently owns the company, which continues to produce competitive racing cars today. The story of Crosslé cars is well told in the book *Hidden Glory* by Alan Tyndall.

ARCHIE FINLAY

Archie Finlay was the youngest son of Alexander Finlay and Matilda Carson of Walmer Terrace, Holywood. It was the grandfather of Alexander Finlay (also Alexander) who had begun the soap-making business in 1798. A stick of shaving soap made in that year was exhibited in London and is still owned by the family.

The business started as soap boilers at Hanover Quay (later Custom House Quay) in Belfast, soon moving to High Street, then to Ann Street and later to Victoria Square where it remained until it closed. The business also expanded to make candles and glycerine, with bonemeal as a by-product. The business became a limited liability company – Alexander Finlay Ltd – about 1905.

Archie Finlay and his brothers Herbert and Robert, together with his nephew Alexander Hugh (Alec) Finlay, managed the soap-making business in its later years until it finally closed in 1949.

The company made a wide range of soaps, including industrial ones for bleachers, finishers, laundries and silk and woollen manufacturers. *Pure Curd* white soap was excellent for washing muslin, while *Pine Tar* soap was effective against skin complaints, and the *Paraffin* soap was used as a strong detergent. In later years *Queen's Pale*, *Silkstone* and *Nimrod* soaps were the most widely used domestic soaps.

Their candles were mostly for domestic use but they also made a special type of candle for Harland & Wolff where they were used while working on ships' hulls, before electric lighting became available.

Alexander Finlay (father of Archie) moved to Holywood when he married Matilda Carson in 1858. They bought the house *Willesden* from John R Neill who had built it a few years previously. *Willesden* was located on the corner of Demesne Road and Church Road – it was demolished at the end of the last century.

In the grounds of *Willesden* there was a polished granite block designed and placed there by Archie Finlay who was a mathematician, on which was engraved a mathematical formula – 'the perfect square'. The family headstone in the Priory graveyard also carries this design on the reverse.

In his retirement Archie Finlay was a keen walker, and was often to be seen around Holywood. He always carried a bag of sweets in his pocket and presented a sweet to each young child he met.

Finlay's factory

Some examples of the soap

SIR PHILIP FOREMAN

Philip Foreman spent much of his life living in Holywood. His contribution to making Shorts aircraft company in Belfast one of the world's leading aerospace companies and a cornerstone of the Northern Ireland economy, was immense.

Philip Foreman was born in Exning, Suffolk, in 1923. He attended Soham Grammar School, from which he won a British Empire Scholarship to Loughborough College. He graduated in 1943, in mechanical engineering.

After graduation, Foreman wanted to join the Royal Navy, but was turned down due to his colour blindness. Instead he joined the Royal Naval Scientific Service, working at the Admiralty Research Laboratory at Teddington. In 1958 he left to join the guided weapon team at Short Brothers and Harland Ltd, where he was initially responsible for all shipborne and depot equipment associated with the Seacat missile weapon system.

In 1961, he became Chief Engineer of the guided weapon division, and in 1964 Company Chief Engineer, responsible for all the Company's engineering activities including aircraft design. He was appointed to the Board in 1965 as Deputy Managing Director and became Managing Director in 1967. In 1983 he became Chairman and Managing Director. Sir Philip had a reputation for being a straight-talking leader who set high standards, but was respected by both his staff and his business competitors.

When Foreman took over the firm, it had accumulated debts of some £12m. The fact that the company had become a *'saleable, surviving entity'* prior to its acquisition by Bombardier was a tribute to the team and to Sir Phil Foreman's leadership of it.

At Short Brothers, Sir Philip consolidated the business into three activities – missiles, aero-structures and aeroplanes, including the development of Skyvan, the 330, 360 and Sherpa. He concentrated particularly on the export market. He was knighted in 1981. In 1985, he became the 100th President of the Institution of Mechanical Engineers.

Sir Philip retired from Shorts in 1988. As well as setting up an engineering consultancy firm, Foreman Associates, he also served as chairman of the British Standards Institution from 1988 to 1991 and as its President from 1994 to 1998. He was made a Freeman of the City of London in 1980 and was awarded an honorary DSc from Queen's University in 1976. He was a Belfast Harbour Commissioner (1974-79) and also a member of the Senate of Queen's University (1993-2002).

In retirement, Sir Philip and his wife Margaret continued to live locally. He passed away on 23 February 2013, Margaret a year later.

BERNARD (BARNEY) HUGHES

Bernard (Barney) Hughes was born in Armagh in 1808. He started work as a baker's boy in 1820 and moved to Belfast in 1826.

By 1833 he was operations manager of the Belfast Public Bakery which was established to prevent unscrupulous private bakers overcharging the working class public. In 1840 his employers threatened that he would lose his job if he attended a dinner in honour of Daniel O'Connell, so he left and opened his own bakery in Donegall Street.

BARNEY
Bernard Hughes of Belfast
1808–1878
Jack Magee

Master baker, Liberal and reformer

The cover of a book on Hughes, *courtesy of the Ulster Historical Foundation*

Hughes' new enterprise flourished and by 1842 was producing £600 worth of bread each week. He opened two further shops in Donegall Place and Divis Street, providing an important staple food for the growing population of urban workers many of whom lacked basic cooking and storage facilities in their overcrowded homes

Given the scale of Hughes' businesses he was in a position to influence, perhaps even control, prices and practices in the baking trade. During the Famine period he kept prices low, and the rural poor, driven to Belfast by hunger and unemployment, looked on bread as a replacement for the potato.

By 1870 Hughes owned the largest baking and milling enterprise in Ireland and was the first elected Roman Catholic Councillor in Belfast. His roles as a municipal politician, industrial reformer and Catholic lay spokesman won him the admiration of all sections of a divided city. He attempted to defuse the bitter sectarian riots in Belfast which brought him into conflict with the Catholic Church and Tory hierarchy, yet gained him respect from both orange and green.

The Hughes family lived in Marine Parade, Holywood before moving to College Square in Belfast. However he always favoured Holywood and brought his employees on holiday excursions to enjoy the sandy beaches. On his retirement in 1868, he came back to Holywood to live in *Riverston House* in Church Road, Holywood, adjacent to the Motte.

He donated the ground on which St Peter's Cathedral was built and donated money to St Mary's Hall in Bank Street. He was also one of the contributors to erect the statue of Dr Henry Cooke, the famous *Black Man* in Wellington Place outside the Royal Belfast Academical Institution, and contributed generously to the building of St Colmcille's Church in Holywood in 1874.

Barney died on 23 September 1878 at *Riverston*. He was buried in Friar's Bush Cemetery at Stranmillis. The third window in the nave of St Colmcille's was dedicated to Bernard Hughes and his wife Jane. (*Riverston* was demolished in 1958.)

SIR SAMUEL KELLY

Sir Samuel Kelly photograph, courtesy of the Ulster History Circle

Samuel Kelly, son of John Kelly (who founded the Coal Company) was born in Castlereagh Street, Belfast in 1880. His grandfather had been a grocer who sold coal; his father had expanded the business and acquired one ship to import his coal.

Samuel was educated at Mountpottinger School and later in the first intake of pupils at Campbell College. He married Mary Stewart from Bangor in 1903 and the following year when his father died, he became company Chairman aged 24. He expanded the company and became a household word. When he died, the fleet of steamers totalled forty, a figure not exceeded by any other coal business.

A Kelly coal boat

In 1921 Samuel bought the Annagher Colliery near Coalisland, and the Cumberland coal mine. He brought two hundred miners from Britain and built houses (Newtownkelly) to accommodate them. He bought two spinning and weaving companies to provide work for the wives. The Coalisland mine was not a success but the local MP in Cumberland said that Sir Samuel Kelly was a model employer.

Samuel was also either the Chairman or a Director of about 20 of Northern Ireland's leading companies. He was a man of action and a sound instinct guided his decisions; his tenacity of purpose was unshakeable.

He took an important if unobtrusive part in Ulster politics being a member of the Ulster Unionist Council. The interests of Northern Irish citizens were well served when he ensured that the supply of coal during the 1926 strike was not interrupted as he negotiated supplies from Europe and America. The extra cost was carried by the Company. The Unionist Party asked him to stand for Parliament in Stormont but he refused on the basis that he had 10,000 employees to look after.

His generosity was unbounded. He was a Methodist, taking an active interest, particularly supporting the building of new churches. He was generous to retired Methodist ministers and to the widows of those who died in service.

Sir Samuel and Lady Kelly had no children and in their later years lived in *Ballymenoch House*, Holywood, and *Stramore* in Donaghadee. He owned a large yacht named *Kelpie,* and was Commodore of Holywood Yacht Club.

He died at the age of 57 in his Holywood home. His widow continued his philanthropy and gave their Holywood home to the Salvation Army for the care of the elderly – the grounds formed what is now Ballymenoch Park. She also provided a new Donaghadee lifeboat named *Sir Samuel Kelly,* which famously went to the rescue of the *Princess Victoria* when she tragically sank in 1953, and is on display at Donaghadee.

MISS MARSH

Miss Annette Marsh was the last member of the Quaker Marsh family who established large biscuit factories in Belfast, with a strong export market. She lived at *Glenlyon*, on Victoria Road, Holywood, a fine house which had been built about 1854. She was a formidable character who did not permit visitors into what was long called Marsh's Glen, at the back of the house; she once even

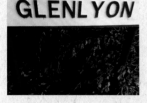

told off a group of Girl Guides who were only looking through the gate!

Her brother, who also lived there, introduced overseas plants such as rhododendrons from the Himalayas. The glen is now an attractive public park with a stream running through it. (The flowers there are very attractive in early summer.)

Local rumour has it that the company invented '*Marshmallows*'. While no proof can be found, it is known that the Marsh family had historical connections with Mallow in County Cork.

One of the Marsh factories was on Upper Donegall Street, near Carrick Hill. The following extracts are from a *1913 Street Directory*:

'*The manufacture of biscuits was introduced into Belfast over 50 years ago, and from a small beginning it has developed into a considerable industry. The trade has been practically in the hands of Marsh & Company, and the fine pile of*

An advertisement for
Marsh's biscuits

buildings in Donegall Street is a striking testimonial to the firm's success. The biscuit trade has provided a wide field of operations for the inventive engineer, and very frequently improved apparatus is introduced, until, at the present moment, the machinery in use by the leading manufacturers has reached a state of perfection almost human in its operations and results.

Marsh's factory is supplied with every modern contrivance for manufacturing biscuits and cakes, from the standard cutting machine to the intricate appliance for the production of "wafers." Over five hundred workers are employed. The trade is extensive, and the firm can compete successfully with English manufacturers for a share of their trade, while the Colonies account for a fair quantity. The Harbour Commissioners' reports for the last few years show that the exports of biscuits from Belfast are usually equal to, and in many cases exceed, the imports; a remarkable fact, when it is remembered that our port is in daily contact with the "Land of Cakes".'

Marsh's vacated the Donegall Street premises in 1930, when a new factory opened on the Springfield Road. The photographer AR Hogg recorded the sophisticated biscuit-cutting machines then installed.

It is also recorded that after the bombing in the Belfast Blitz in 1941 people were served from the warehouses of Marsh's biscuit factory.

ALEXANDER MITCHELL

Alexander Mitchell was a remarkable engineer who deserves to be much better-known.

Former beacon off Cultra

He was born in Dublin in 1780, as one of 13 children, but the family then moved to Belfast. His father died when he was 10; losing his sight in his teens, he was totally blind by the age of 22.

In Belfast, Mitchell set up a brick works, but his main claim to fame was as an inventor and engineer.

In the 1830s, first in Belfast Lough, he devised the screw pile which would enable the construction of a platform on sandbanks as the basis for a light beacon (or light-house). Large cast iron screws were attached to the bottom of 20 feet long wooden (or later iron) piles which were then bored into the sand using a temporary capstan. The light beacon erected on top saved ships from running aground or sinking on unmarked sandbanks.

In 1844, at a cost of £1,300, Mitchell erected a screw pile light-house on Holywood Bank in Belfast Lough which was to serve as a beacon and a permanently-manned pilot station. Once, when going to the Holywood beacon, Mitchell – being blind – fell into the sea. His son, who was his helper, recorded that he came up *'cool and collected, with his hat lost but his stick in his right hand'*. According to some accounts

A Mitchell light beacon at Moville

the original erection suffered damage in 1889, but a pile light-house continued in the Lough off Craigavad until the 1950s (when it was briefly replaced with the light-ship now at Ballydorn).

There are several extant Mitchell light beacons in Ireland – one stands in Lough Foyle off Moville. The one in Cork Harbour, marking the Spit Bank was erected in 1851; a large-scale model, with the original red light at its top, can be seen on the main street in Cobh. Mitchell's innovative system was used to erect beacons and jetties across the world, including in India and America.

Mitchell was also one of the inventors of the screw propeller which he patented in 1854. He generously granted the General Screw Steamship Company the free use of his invention in all their ships.

In 1854, he moved to Victoria Terrace in Holywood, and later he went to live with his daughter Margaret, at *Farmhill House* at Marino. He died in 1868, and was buried in Clifton Street graveyard.

Mitchell was also an excellent musician and an authority on Irish music. As one contemporary wrote, when one considered his handicap, his *'conduct was to be eulogised, and his ingenuity and perseverance were to be admired'*.

MARGARET ROSE MOUNTFORD

Born on 24 November 1951, *Margaret Mountford* is a British lawyer, businesswoman and television personality best known for her role in *The Apprentice.*

Originally from Holywood in Northern Ireland, the daughter of High Street Presbyterian Minister Ross Gamble and his wife Kathleen, she was educated at Strathearn Grammar School in Belfast, then at Girton College, Cambridge. Returning to education later in life, she completed her PhD in 2012 at University College, London.

Mrs Mountford spent a number of years as a lawyer with Herbert Smith, before taking on roles as non-executive director at Amstrad and Essenden. She is currently chairman of Argent Foods Limited, a private group of companies with operations mainly in the food sector, and also chairs the board of governors of St Marylebone CE Bridge School, a free school for pupils with special needs in speech, language and communication, and the Egypt Exploration Society, a charity founded in 1882 to sponsor and carry out fieldwork and research on ancient and mediaeval Egypt, and its publication.

From 2005 to 2009, Mrs Mountford was one of Lord Sugar's advisers, alongside Nick Hewer, in the UK version of *The Apprentice* television show, a role in which she achieved increasing public popularity.

She left the show in 2009 to return to her studies, and in 2012 she finished her PhD in Papyrology at University College London (the study of ancient documents written on papyrus). Margaret specialised in documents from the Roman and Byzantine periods.

She appeared in an episode of the 2010 series, where she helped Lord Sugar narrow down the candidates to a final two, and had a similar role in the 2012 and 2013 series.

Margaret has made a number of appearances on Channel 4's *Countdown*, hosted by Nick Hewer, as a guest in Dictionary Corner. She has presented documentaries for the BBC on Pompeii, the ancient Greek poet Sappho and the photographer Harry Burton, most famous for his work with Howard Carter, photographing the contents of Tutankamun's tomb.

With Nick Hewer, she co-presented four BBC documentaries, focussing on the challenges involved in people having to continue working later in life, the benefits culture, immigration and the railways.

In October 2013, she presented a BBC Two Northern Ireland documentary called *Ground-breakers: Ulster's Forgotten Radical*, which highlighted the forgotten women's rights campaigner from the 19th century, Isabella Tod.

WILLIAM ADOLPHUS ROSS

Born in Dublin in 1817, William was the only son of Henry and Catherine Ross. Following his mother's death in 1827 his father moved the family to Belfast. After leaving school, William joined his father in John Kane's brewery in North Street where Henry was employed as manager, so laying the seeds of knowledge which would stand him in good stead at a later stage in his career.

Following Kane's death in 1847 the brewery was sold. However, William and two partners purchased another one of Kane's businesses, the Shamrock Glass Works at Short Strand; within a short time he was in sole control of it. Unfortunately the business, like all previous attempts to manufacture glass in the area, did not succeed and was wound up by 1865. Around 1860 William and his wife Frances had settled in Holywood, at Marine Parade. Recognising his precarious business situation, they moved to London in 1863, where William re-engaged with his brewing roots.

In 1869, the offer of a job to manage Cantrell & Cochrane's new aerated water factory in Police Square (now Victoria Square) drew him back to Belfast. Under his guidance the business became a roaring success. In 1879, following a difference of opinion, William left Cantrell & Cochrane and set up a rival firm, WA Ross & Co. in the stable yard of a hotel in William Street South, next door to his old employer. A new factory (now Argos) was soon erected and a deep artesian well, a key ingredient in ensuring the quality of the firm's products, was sunk. Ross's went from strength to strength.

William's son George (who had spent twenty years at sea) became his right hand man and his other two sons, who acted as agents in America, switched their allegiance from Cantrell & Cochrane to the new enterprise. Within a short time Ross's became, as its advertising slogan trumpeted, '*favourably known all over the world*'. The two best known products were its Pale Dry and Royal Belfast Ginger Ales. Another speciality was Ross's Raspberry Vinegar, prepared from a special class of berry grown at William's residence, *The Ivies* at Craigavad. Following his wife's death in 1885, William purchased a small property, also at Craigavad, where he built some houses, one of which, *Iva-Craig*, he lived in until his death in 1900. He was buried in the family plot in the Old Priory Graveyard.

JOHN GETTY McGEE AND CATHERINE ELIZABETH McGEE

John Getty McGee, born in Antrim in 1816, was in his teens when he obtained an apprenticeship with J Holden's Hat Emporium in Belfast's High Street; by 1831 he was managing the business, and in 1838 took it over.

JOHN C. M'CEE & Co.,
MERCHANT CLOTHIERS,
EMBROIDERED VEST MANUFACTURERS,
ROBE AND GOWN MAKERS,
(For the Pulpit, the Bar, or the College.)
TAILORS, BY APPOINTMENT,
TO THE QUEEN, H.R.H. PRINCE ALBERT,
THE LORD LIEUTENANT OF IRELAND.
General Out-fitters to all parts of the Globe.
PANTECHNETHECA,
46 & 48 HIGH STREET, BELFAST.
*Books of Prices, containing directions for Measures; also Patterns
of New Materials, forwarded Gratis on application.*

THE
"ULSTER" OVERCOAT

THE ORIGINAL IRISH PRIZE
DRIVING AND TRAVELLING WRAP.
Patterns of Materials, and all Instructions for Self-Measurement, with
Illustrated Catalogue, forwarded on application.

M'GEE & CO., BELFAST, IRELAND.

His insistence on the highest standards of craftsmanship and quality soon bore fruit. He expanded the range and specialised: in 1852 he boasted of *'the largest stock of winter overcoats in the north of Ireland'*. The greatcoat was then an essential part of the traveller's wardrobe but was heavy and cumbersome. McGee set himself the task of designing a modern travelling coat. It would be a dozen years and more, before he introduced it in 1866.

Success swiftly followed and the word *ulster* was soon imported into many languages, outperforming its inventor's most ambitious expectations. For the next sixty years the firm promoted itself as *'inventors and sole makers of the ulster coat'* (proudly acknowledging the fact that it been pirated by virtually every tailor in the civilised world).

The trade journal *Tailor & Cutter* said 'No gentleman's wardrobe is complete without an ulster'. Though originally designed for men, a female version of *'the best storm defier ever produced'* was soon introduced. It was also imported into literature and films – Sherlock Holmes was an ulster wearer.

In 1855, McGee organised the Holywood Wharf Scheme to provide a new jetty for the sea front (at a cost of £257, it was 150ft long). The first sign of him living in Holywood was in 1860/61 at Marine Parade. By 1865 he resided at *Spafield*, High Street, where he lived until his death in 1883. He was actively involved in civic, church and Masonic affairs. Following his funeral at Holywood Parish Church, he was buried in the family vault in the Old Priory Graveyard.

McGee's greatest source of pride and possibly his lasting legacy, was that he had introduced a new word, with derivatives, to dictionaries. (The ulster is more correctly spelt with a small "u".)

His daughter, **Catherine Elizabeth McGee,** was born in 1849. Catherine played a central role in the development of women's golf in Ireland. She first visited the Belfast Golf Club at Kinnegar in 1887 where she met an officer's wife playing golf, who inspired her to play the game. The following year, she arranged an inaugural meeting of Lady Golfers in Holywood, and in 1893, she convened a meeting in Belfast which created the Irish Ladies Golf Union – according to one source, the oldest such national union in the world.

DOCTOR ARCHIBALD DUNLOP, AND SWEENEY'S PHARMACY

Archibald Dunlop was born in County Antrim. On completing his medical degree at Queen's College, Belfast, he came to live in Holywood in a house he had built – *St Helen's* on the High Street – where he set up his medical practice. A local dispensary was established in 1850 and in 1857 Dr Dunlop was appointed as its Medical Officer. He was the Medical Officer of Health for the District for 44 years.

He was instrumental in setting up "The Society for Nursing the Sick Poor of Holywood" in 1883 and succeeded in building a residence for the District Nurses in Holywood in Church Street (now Road), by public subscription. It was named *'The Dunlop Memorial Home'* at a later date. The Home was sold in 1957, as it was deemed no longer necessary, due to the advent of the National Health Service and the Welfare State. (It is now the Abbeyfield Home.)

St Helen's today

Dr Dunlop was a magistrate at Holywood Petty Sessions Court and a governor of Sullivan School.

He died on 13 November 1902 at *St Helen's*. He had been a prominent member of Holywood Parish Church and a memorial was erected there.

Two of the sons of Dr Dunlop were killed in the Great War. 2nd Lieutenant John Gunning Moore Dunlop was one of the first two men from North Down to die on the Western Front, on 27 August 1914. His brother, Captain George Malcolm Dunlop died at Gallipoli on 25 April 1915. Their mother, Bessie Dunlop, unveiled the Holywood and District War Memorial in Redburn Square on 28 January 1922.

SWEENEY'S PHARMACY

In the early 1870s, John Payne established a medical hall in High Street, Holywood. In 1895, he moved to Holywood, at 10 High Street. By 1906, Payne retired, and his medical hall was taken over by JS Scott. By 1914, his practice ceased to be known as a medical hall and Charles Sweeney was a chemist at 62, High Street.

The front of Sweeney's pharmacy

Mr Sweeney appears to have taken over Scott's practice about 1918, being recorded at 52 High Street. Charles Sweeney died in 1942, and his wife, Mrs Audrey Sweeney took over the business, which was managed by Miss Meneely. By this time, the chemist's shop was at no. 50 (the present address), with Mrs Sweeney residing at no. 52. In 1953 the firm became known as Sweeney's Pharmacies Ltd. Kenneth Dickson bought the practice in November 1972.

THE DUNVILLE FAMILY

Violet Dunville in one of the family's hot air balloons

Some have said that the Dunvilles were 'Holywood's Royal Family'. In 1866 Robert Grimshaw Dunville built *Redburn House*, when he was only 28 years old.

Six years earlier, his Uncle William gave him a partnership in the family's Whiskey Distillery in Belfast, alongside James Craig (father of Northern Ireland's first Prime Minister). Robert was a Justice of the Peace, a Deputy Lieutenant of Co. Down, a High Sheriff of County Meath, a founder of the Reform Club and a member of the Liberal Party – until the British Prime Minister, William Gladstone, advocated Home Rule for Ireland. Robert then became a Liberal Unionist, and a friend of the Duke of Devonshire

2nd Lieutenant John Spencer Dunville VC

who founded the Liberal Unionist Party and Robert's son, John, became private secretary to the Duke.

When his father died in 1910, John (hereafter referred to as Colonel John) took over as Chairman of Dunville's Whiskey Distillery. In 1892, Colonel John married Violet Lambart, grand-daughter of the Marquis of Conyngham of Beau Park, County Meath. He and his wife were great balloonists. They had four children; three sons were educated at Eton while their daughter who had learning disabilities was sent to Normansfield Hospital in Teddington, Middlesex where she remained until her death in 1958. Her brothers all served as soldiers during the First World War, while Colonel John was one of the few to hold officer rank in all three Services, (as Colonel of the West Meath Militia, Squadron Commander in the Royal Naval Air Service and Wing Commander in the Royal Air Force).

But the War period brought much sadness to the Dunville family. Their eldest son, Bobby, was travelling to Kingstown (Dun Laoghaire) to return to his regiment in April 1916 when his car was ambushed at Castlebellingham, and he was shot in the chest, during the Easter Rising. Consequently he suffered from poor physical health and died aged 38. In June 1917, their second son, 2nd Lieutenant John, was killed in action (for which he was posthumously awarded the Victoria Cross). After the war, their youngest son, William (also called Gustavus Adolphus) emigrated to Australia and later to Canada.

When Colonel John died in 1929, Bobby succeeded in the family business until his death in 1931. In 1935 the Directors of the Distillery stopped Grain Spirit Distilling *'because of overstocking'*. The stock of whiskey and other assets were sold over the subsequent 12 years.

Violet Dunville remained a much admired figure in the town and she continued to live in *Redburn House* until her death in 1940.

REVEREND CANON ERIC S BARBER

Eric Skottowe Barber was born in Dublin in 1911 and educated at St Andrew's and Trinity College where he took an honours degree in classics. He later entered Divinity School.

In 1935 he was ordained by the then Church of Ireland Bishop of Down, John McNeice, for the curacy of St Mary Magdalene in Donegall Pass. Two years later he moved to Bangor remaining there for three years before leaving for an eight month rectorship of St James on the Antrim Road, Belfast.

In September 1945 he was instituted as vicar of Holywood Parish where he remained for the next 40 years. However, despite staying in one parish, his talents reached far and wide and he had important roles in both the Church of Ireland and as a representative on various church and television bodies. These included being appointed a Canon of St Patrick's Cathedral in Dublin, and as Archdeacon of Down in 1973.

Canon Barber once commented that he found his involvement with the media *'tremendously exciting'*. He was the Church of Ireland adviser to UTV and, following this, he was the Irish representative on the religious panel of the ITA (now IBA). He made over 100 television appearances and from Holywood Parish 50 BBC broadcasts were made during his time there.

Canon Barber was also a keen sportsman. He was captain of Trinity College cricket team in 1935 and later played cricket for North, Cliftonville, Bangor and Holywood. He was a former Leinster Senior Inter-Provincial cricketer. Hockey was his other sport, and as well as playing for his University, he played for Lisnagarvey, Bangor and Holywood.

His outside interests were not confined to sport. He had a love of music and was vice-president of the Holywood Music Festival Committee for many years; his wife, Maureen, was Honorary Secretary.

Canon Barber's ministry in Holywood Parish was one of total commitment to his parishioners and from such a commitment sprang the enthusiasm and energy of a loving servant of God. He took great interest and pleasure in those he had baptised and prepared for confirmation, and in some cases performed their marriage ceremonies and even baptised their children.

The Barbers' four children shared their parents' musical abilities and talents.

Canon Barber died in 1985. The people of Holywood who knew him, either through the parish church, music festivals or the sporting scene, remember him with gratitude for the contribution he gave to the town.

BISHOP KEN CLARKE

Bishop Ken Clarke was born on 23 May 1949 and grew up in Holywood. He was the only child of Herbie and Anne Clarke. He attended Holywood Nursery School, Holywood Primary School and Sullivan Upper where he was a Senior Prefect, Captain of the First XV in 1966-67, an active member of the Scripture Union and a keen actor in the annual school plays.

Bishop Ken was ordained in 1972 after graduating from Trinity College Dublin and the Church of Ireland Theological College. In 1971 he married Cork girl Helen Good and they have 4 daughters and 5 grandchildren. (He is often known by his nickname Fanta, which he has had since he was 11 years old.)

He was Curate in Magheralin and Dundonald. In February 1979 he, Helen and the family began life as Mission Partners with the South American Mission Society (SAMS) in Valdivia, Chile. From 1982-86 he was Incumbent of Crinken Church in Dublin before becoming Rector of St Patrick's Coleraine, (where he succeeded Canon Jim Monroe who had moved to St Philip and St James Holywood).

He was Rector of Coleraine Parish for 15 years and Archdeacon of Dalriada for several years. In November 2000 he became Church of Ireland Bishop of Kilmore, Elphin and Ardagh and lived in Cavan for 12 years. During that time he was Chairperson of Cavan Royal School.

From January 2013 to July 2018 he was Mission Director of SAMS in Ireland and has travelled extensively in South America. He has led Missions, Retreats, and preached at Conferences and Conventions in different parts of the world including Singapore, Malaysia, Africa, New Zealand and South America. In 2013 and in April 2016 he gave the Bible Readings at the New Wineskins Missions Conference in the USA, a conference with over 1,000 people from 40 different countries.

He is also the author of *Going For Growth* published by IVP which is about learning lessons for life and leadership from the apostle Peter. He has also contributed to several other books.

Bishop Ken has a particular interest in church growth and leadership issues. He claims not to be retired but refired, and says he prioritises *FLIP – 'Family and Friends... Learning more... Investing in younger leaders... Preaching and teaching'*.

REVEREND HAROLD GOOD

Harold Good was born in April 1937 in Londonderry where his father was the Superintendent of the Methodist Derry City Mission.

At the age of four, he was smitten with bovine tuberculosis for which the only known treatment was to immobilise the spine totally. For the next three years Harold was strapped to an iron frame and lay flat on his back on a home-made wooden trolley. Harold was home-schooled by his mother until he could walk.

When he was nearly nine, his father was transferred to Newtownards Road Methodist Church. Harold started formal schooling at Strandtown Primary. He caught up sufficiently to pass the "Qually" which gave him entry into First Form at Methodist College.

As the son of a Methodist minister, the family's life centred around the church, in which at the moment of confirmation Harold was to make a conscious and personal commitment to follow the way of Christ. Before leaving school he decided to offer himself as a candidate for the Methodist ministry.

This ministry took Harold on journeys he could never have anticipated. This included four years of serving and learning in the USA, returning to Ireland in 1968 to serve as Minister in the Shankill Road at the beginning of the Troubles. This was to be the beginning of a lifetime ministry of reconciliation, part of this as Director of the Corrymeela Centre, as well as Circuit ministry in provincial and city churches.

This 'ministry of reconciliation' involved Harold, with others, in the building of relationships with and between people who were deeply involved politically and/or physically in conflict. While most of this was 'back stage', there were times when what was known was neither understood nor appreciated! For Harold this ministry of reconciliation was deeply rooted in his understanding of the Gospel.

It was in the building of these relationships of trust that, in 2005, Father Alex Reid and Harold were asked to play a pivotal role in witnessing the de-commissioning of the weaponry of the PIRA. This was followed by involvement in the peace process in the Basque Country, as well as with the exiled leadership of FARC in Cuba and in Colombia. For Harold, it was an unforgettable moment when, together with the Roman Catholic Archbishop of Bologne, he was asked to play a significant role in the de-commissioning of the weapons of ETA, bringing to an end the longest running civil conflict in Europe.

Harold has been married to Clodagh for 54 years; they live in Holywood. They have five children and twelve grandchildren.

LAISRÉN Mac NASCA (SAINT LAISREN)

This holy man is best known as the founder of the ancient Priory in Holywood, which he completed around the year 635. The Irish name for the town is called after him, *Ard Mhic Nasca*, The Height of Nasca's Son. The many old calendars of the Irish saints give his commemoration date as 25 October and use phrases such as 'the great Laisrén son of Nasca' and 'the holy Laisrén son of Nasca', and he is described as 'Laisrén, son of Nasca, of Ard Mhic Nasca on the shore of Loch Laoigh (now called Belfast Lough) in Ulster'.

He had trained for the clergy under Saint Mochuda, (also called Carthach) a Munsterman who himself had spent some time as a student with St Comgall

in Bangor. It is likely that it was in the Bangor monastery that Mochuda got to know Laisrén and his brothers, Goban and Srafan, who all went with him on his return to Munster, having studied under his care in the monastery of Rathyne. They were then put in charge of

A postcard of the Old Priory

the monastery which Mochuda had established in Spike Island about 620. Saint Goban was ordained bishop and placed in charge of that monastery, while Laisrén returned to Ulster where he managed his Priory at Holywood.

At this time a controversy raged in monastic Ireland about the differences between Ireland and Rome over a number of liturgical practices. The main issues were the date of the celebration of Easter, and the form of monastic tonsure. Rome was beginning to insist that Ireland and its satellite institutions in Iona and in Northumbria should conform to the Roman customs, but were meeting great resistance, especially from Ulster, Scotland and the north of England. There was no general agreement until the Synod of Whitby in 664. In the meantime the southern Irish monasteries had begun to conform, but the northern clergy, including Laisrén, continued to resist. A letter from the Roman clergy in 642 to Laisrén and ten other named leading Ulster clerics was concerned about their non-compliance and the dangers of the Pelagian heresy.

At one time there was a crescent of monasteries in North Down, also including Knock, Bangor, Movilla, Nendrum and Greyabbey.

It is likely that the area of the Priory extended up to Brook Street, and may have taken in the hill of the Motte. Its location close to the Ballykeel river provided scope for a water mill. It was here that Holywood really took root, and it is thus to Laisrén that the town owes its origins.

REVEREND CJ McALESTER

Reverend CJ McAlester was born in 1810. He was educated at the Belfast Academical Institution, where he then became a master. He continued to have a deep interest in education all his life.

In August 1834 he was inducted into the ministry to the Non-Subscribing Presbyterian church in Holywood. At that time the congregation was meeting in the old Shore Road church where the Reverend McAlester founded a school.

In 1849 the congregation moved to the handsome new church in High Street. Here, he established a very well-attended Sunday school and preparatory school for boys and girls. The school was held in two

Portrait by Anthony Carey Stannus

rooms underneath the church and below the level of the High Street. Locally it became known as the '*Underground Academy*'. Some of the distinguished students were James Craig (who became Lord Craigavon), Sir Dawson Bates, Rosamond Praeger and her brother Robert Lloyd Praeger, which says much for the excellence of the school.

Reverend McAlester was a close friend of Robert Sullivan, founder of the Sullivan Schools. He became a founder member of, and secretary to, the Board of Management of Sullivan Upper School. Today there is a Sullivan 'school house' named after him.

The McAlester memorial obelisk in front of Holywood's Non-Subscribing Presbyterian church

The Reverend McAlester was on friendly terms with the clergy of all denominations in the Holywood area, including Father O'Laverty. His long ministry brought him membership of many social committees in the town. Con Auld wrote that in 1835 he became a member of the Parish Vestry and remained a member until 1869.

He was the editor of *The Bible Christian* and Clerk of the Northern Presbytery until his death, after 57 years of ministry in Holywood, in 1891. (In 1867, he threatened to resign, due to his meagre salary, but the members of the congregation persuaded him to stay on.) He spoke fluent Irish.

One author has opined that no other resident has given a greater life of service to the town.

An obelisk in the forecourt of the Non-Subscribing Presbyterian church on High Street was erected in his memory, paid for by Christians across Holywood. A portrait of him in 1884 by another Holywood resident, the painter, Anthony Carey Stannus, hangs in the vestibule of the church.

MONSIGNOR JAMES O'LAVERTY

James O'Laverty is noted most for his five-volume account of the history of the Diocese of Down and Connor (written in 1878-87). He is fondly remembered for his inspiring pastoral work in the parish of Colmcille in Holywood, and he took an enthusiastic and influential part in the Gaelic Revival.

He was born in Carrowbane, Killough on 22 November 1828; he entered St Malachy's College (Diocesan Seminary) in 1844 and, after three years, was admitted to Maynooth College. His first parish was Ahoghill and Portglenone where he was appointed curate in 1852. He spent five years in that parish before he joined St Malachy's College where he was Dean.

In 1866 he was made Parish Priest of Holywood where he spent the next 40 years. Imbued with a deep sense of identity and a strong pride of place, he built up a sizeable literary output, and collections of archaeological artefacts, of Gaelic manuscripts and of rare Irish books. A fellow Celtophile, FJ Bigger said about him, '*He had travelled much .... But his deepest affection was for the tongue of the Gael. It had a depth and beauty of meaning that seemed to meet the very fullness of his soul.*'

Even before the formation of the Gaelic League (in 1893), O'Laverty had been a member of the Council of the Gaelic Union which published *Irisleabhar na Gaeilge* (Gaelic Journal) founded in 1882 to preserve and cultivate the Irish language. Soon after the formation of the League he was elected as one of the Vice-Presidents of the Belfast Branch.

His learned contributions were acknowledged by his being made a Member of the Royal Irish Academy (1869), and his Church conferred on him the title of Monsignor.

In his own parish he brought together a community, built for them a fine church (on a site obtained from Captain Harrison) to replace the old chapel in Church View and started, in 1902, a branch of the Gaelic League. He also established a school in Holywood – St Laiseran's Academy on Ean Hill, in 1874. It closed three years later (for lack of pupils) so he converted it into his residence.

He was quick to acknowledge the assistance he received in his historical research from others, particularly the Anglican Bishop William Reeves. The History of the Parish of Holywood was also printed separately – an early historical account of the town in book form.

When he died in April 1906, his remains were buried in a grave just outside the church which he had designed. His portrait, painted by Holywood artist Cecilia Harrison (1863-1941), is in the Ulster Museum.

PATRICK MacNAMEE (PÁDRAIG Mac CONMIDHE)

Patrick MacNamee was born in Carrickastickan, Co. Armagh in 1896 and graduated as a teacher from De La Salle Training College, Waterford. He later obtained his BA with honours and his MA from London University and spent the last 20 years of his teaching career as Principal of St Patrick's Primary School, Holywood.

He was a life-long member of the Gaelic League and was twice President of the All Ireland Organisation. He was honoured for his sterling work on behalf of the Irish language by being elected the first President of the umbrella organisation of all Irish Language groups in Ireland, Comhdháil Náisunta na Gaeilge (established in 1943).

For many years Patrick MacNamee lectured in Irish at St Mary's College of Education in Belfast. He was chief examiner in both O and A level Irish for the Department of Education until his retirement, after which he took a keen interest in the affairs of the Northern Ireland Retired Teachers' Association, in which he served as Chairman and Secretary.

He was a prolific writer of books and textbooks in Irish and was a regular contributor to the *Irish Weekly News*. When Radio Éireann was established, he was appointed a member of the Authority.

In 1921, the Holywood Irish Society, a branch of Comhaltas Uladh (Ulster Gaelic League) was formed. Patrick MacNamee was the secretary. The Society is still thriving and holds an annual festival in the town in March.

He wrote a history of the town, entitled *The History of Holywood*, which was strong on the years before 1800.

During his life time he took an active part in the GAA (Gaelic Athletic Association) and was President from 1938 to 1943. He also served as Chairman of the Ulster Council on two occasions.

He died at his home, *Bláithín*, My Lady's Mile, Holywood on 28 March 1975 and is buried in Holywood Cemetery.

The MacNamee Awards – the GAA National Communication and Media

THE HISTORY OF HOLYWOOD
by P. MacNamee M.A.

Awards – were named after him. They are presented annually in recognition of outstanding contributions by individuals and associations in these areas. When presenting the 2016 awards, the GAA President, Aogán Ó Fearghail said, '*The late Pádraig MacNamee was a man ahead of his time in many ways and it is fitting that these awards should be named in his honour*'.

ROBERT SULLIVAN

Robert Sullivan was born in a cottage on High Street, Holywood, on 3 January 1800, the son of a Kerry man who was stationed locally in the Revenue Service and married a Holywood girl. Showing great academic promise, the young Robert Sullivan was admitted to the newly-opened Royal Belfast Academical Institution, having been nominated by a local landowner, Mr Cunningham Greg of Ballymenoch.

After a successful school career, Sullivan entered Trinity College, Dublin. He was selected as an Inspector of Schools in May 1832; one of four appointed by the National Board of Education for the whole of Ireland. He then began to write a series of school text books on subjects such as spelling, English grammar, and geography

The bust of Robert Sullivan by the Irish sculptor Joseph Watkins (at Sullivan Upper School)

and an English dictionary. The Sullivan textbooks were used throughout the English-speaking world and became the basis for his considerable wealth.

In 1838 he was promoted to the office of Superintendent or Professor of the Teacher Training Department in Marlborough Street, Dublin. Through this and the use of his textbooks, his lessons were studied throughout the island of Ireland. He was called to the Bar in 1838 and obtained the degree of LLD from Trinity College, Dublin in 1858.

A generous man throughout his life, Dr Sullivan made numerous donations to educational causes including his old school, Queen's College, Belfast and National Schools all over Ireland. He firmly worked towards a type of schooling founded in Christian principles but essentially non-sectarian in nature.

In 1859 he entrusted to the son of his early benefactor Mr Greg the sum of two thousand pounds for the erection and endowment of a National School (for boys and girls) in Holywood. The original school building, which was designed by Lanyon, Lynn and Lanyon, opened in 1862.

After his death in 1868 the trustees of his will were required to pass on more of his bequests to educational causes. He left a similar sum for the further benefit of the Sullivan National Schools in Holywood.

Thus Sullivan Upper School came into being in 1877 (including the iconic clock-tower) physically conjoined with the earlier facility for primary schoolchildren. The whole building, now beautifully restored and serving as the town's library, remains. Sullivan Upper School moved to its current premises in 1940, where it not only bears the Sullivan name, family motto and coat of arms but also subscribes to his principles of non-denominational education.

This successful voluntary grammar school, now with over one thousand pupils is one of the most tangible reminders of the life of this remarkable educationalist whose remains reside in the Old Priory Graveyard.

PETER WOODMAN

Peter Charles Woodman, who was born in 1943 and died aged 73, was Emeritus Professor of Archaeology at University College, Cork (UCC). With 113

publications to his name, he was the leading authority on the Irish Mesolithic period during which the first settlers arrived in Ireland after 8,000 BC. He was also the former assistant keeper of prehistoric antiquities at the Ulster Museum, Belfast.

Remarkably, at UCC, Peter Woodman PhD, DLitt (QUB) also taught t'ai chi, an ancient form of non-competitive Chinese martial arts, aimed at reducing stress and keeping fit.

In a glowing tribute to his scholarly work as an archaeologist, Professor Jim Mallory of QUB, described him as its most illustrious archaeology graduate, adding that his research work provided

At Queen's University, Belfast

'the basic structure of all subsequent research into the Irish Mesolithic'.

He inspired several generations of archaeologists through his passion for his subject, his readiness to challenge accepted 'facts' and his quirky wit.

Shortly after his appointment as professor of archaeology in Cork in 1983, he published an account of his excavations at Mount Sandel in County Londonderry, the earliest dated Mesolithic settlement structures in Ireland. Up to that point, as Professor Mallory put it, the Irish Mesolithic was essentially 'a northern affair' but this changed when Peter set out to search for evidence in Munster. His excavations at Ferriter's Cove in Co Kerry uncovered fascinating evidence about the last foragers and first farmers on the Dingle Peninsula.

In 2009 he was awarded the Europa prize by the Prehistoric Society for his outstanding contribution to European history. His magnum opus, *Ireland's First Settlers*, encompassed 50 years of personal experience searching to make sense of what initially '*appeared to be little more than a collection of beach-rolled and battered flint tools*'. It tells the story of the archaeology and history of the first continuous phase of Ireland's human settlement.

Professor Woodman gives a vivid account of how the story of the first settlers was embedded in the position, landscape and ecology of the island of Ireland and how that impacted on when and how it was colonised in the period from 8,000 to 4,500 BC. Suggesting that they probably arrived on the north-east coast from Scotland, he explores how their way of life evolved to suit the narrow range of resources available.

Full of intellectual curiosity since his boyhood days in Holywood, Peter encouraged his students to indulge in '*the pleasure of finding things out*'. He had a knack of making people feel that their contribution mattered.

His wife recalls '*Peter loved Holywood. He felt it's where his roots were*'.

SIR ROBERT LLOYD PATTERSON

The bust by Rosamond Praeger in Holywood Library

Robert Lloyd Patterson was born in College Square, Belfast in December 1836, one of eleven children. By profession a linen manufacturer, he was also an important amateur naturalist and art collector. He is of interest in Holywood both in his own right and as the uncle of Rosamond and Robert Lloyd Praeger.

His mother was a poet, while his father, Robert, had been a mill-owner, and (in 1821, at the age of just 18 years) an initial founder of the Belfast Natural History Society. Robert senior wrote several books, including *Zoology for Schools*. He was awarded the Templeton medal, instituted by the Society. (Interestingly he was in the museum of the Natural History Society when the first mummy to arrive in Belfast was unrolled – it had been donated by Thomas Greg of Ballymenoch in Holywood.)

Young Robert, after learning German and French on the continent, was apprenticed to the linen firm of Praeger and Company, in 1852. He set up his own flax, tow and yarn company in Belfast at just 21, through which he became wealthy. He served later as President of the Belfast Chamber of Commerce. John Haynes-Williams painted Patterson's portrait in 1897.

He was a founding member of the Belfast Naturalists' Field Club. In 1880 he published a book entitled *Birds, Fishes and Cetacea of Belfast Lough*. Robert Lloyd Praeger described his uncle as his '*first tutor in natural science*'. Robert's brother, William, wrote *A Glossary of Words and Phrases used in Antrim and Down*.

He married in 1861, and in 1888, in his retirement, Robert Lloyd Patterson came to live in *Croft House;* (the Praeger family were then living next door in *Woodburn House*). PRONI has a large document, setting out in precise detail, the alterations that he wanted made to *Croft House*, eg '*the bricks were to be best Bangor or Belfast compressed…*'. Although childless, he took a keen interest in the Praeger children, helping to pay for their education.

He received a knighthood for his civic services in 1902, and died in January 1906. He bequeathed his collection of Victorian paintings to Belfast Corporation – it is now in the Ulster Museum. He supported the development of a natural history or Patterson Museum, named after his father, to which he donated his array of stuffed birds and mammals.

Holywood Library has a bust of Patterson on display which was sculpted by Rosamond Praeger.

JOHN TEMPLETON, WILLIAM HENRY PHILLIPS AND ROBERT LLOYD PRAEGER

Holywood has had some remarkable botanists and natural historians – both amateur and professional.

The district was also the location of the discovery of famous wild Irish Rose, *rosa hibernica*.

The discovery, in 1795, is attributed to **John Templeton** who described it as a new species. He was awarded a prize of five guineas from the Royal Dublin Society. According to some accounts, the first specimen was found in what is now the new Priory graveyard, on an embankment, although Knocknagoney is the more often-cited location. The rose was called both the 'Holywood rose' and 'Templeton's rose'.

William Henry Phillips (1831-1921) lived at *Lemonfield* in Holywood. In 1877 he discovered a new form of soft-shield fern, to which his name was given. Phillips was a distinguished botanist, but his real love was ferns, many of which he grew in the grounds of his house. He was President of the British Pteridological Society in 1904-5, the head of a linen firm in Albert Street, and also a prominent freemason. His funeral procession to Holywood parish church was said to be '*the largest seen in that area in living memory*'.

One of the best known Irish naturalists is **Robert Lloyd Praeger** (1865-1953), the older brother of the sculptor, Rosamond. Like her, he attended the school of the Reverend McAlester, and then Sullivan Upper School. They were both leading members of the Belfast Naturalists' Field Club.

He worked in the National Library of Ireland in Dublin from 1893 to 1923. He co-founded and edited the *Irish Naturalist*, and wrote papers on the flora and other aspects of the natural history of Ireland. He organised the Lambay Survey in 1905-06 and, from 1909 to 1915, the wider Clare Island Survey. He was an engineer by qualification, a librarian by profession and a naturalist by inclination.

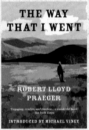

His best known book was *The Way that I Went: An Irishman in Ireland*, a lyrical guide to the natural history of the island of Ireland, published in 1937.

He was awarded the Veitch Memorial Medal of the Royal Horticultural Society in 1921. He became the first President of both An Taisce and the Irish Mountaineering Club in 1948, and served as President of the Royal Irish Academy for 1931–34.

He spent his last year living with his sister at Cultra, and is buried in Deansgrange Cemetery, Dublin with his wife Hedwig.

REVEREND JOHN McCONNELL AULD

Con Auld was born in *Clanbrassil,* his grandmother's home in Cultra, on 15 September 1929. His father was a captain of the Belfast Head Line Shipping Company. His mother's family (Morrow) had come to *Clanbrassil* in the late 19th century, while the Aulds were in Holywood by 1841.

Con attended the new kindergarten of Sullivan Upper School on Holywood High Street. He then transferred to Belfast Royal Academy where he held a Maxwell Scholarship.

After graduating from Trinity College Dublin, Con gained a Danforth scholarship to Princeton, New Jersey, USA. The Korean War was then in progress. Con was a member of the Princeton Choir and the US Department of Defence declared all choir members to be '*thru captains*' in the US Army, sending them to Korea and Japan to entertain the forces.

Later, a McCaw Missionary Scholarship took him to Union College in Belfast for ordination to the Presbyterian Church. Con's first parish was in Goodwood in Adelaide, Australia. Returning after a three year stay, he joined the staff of the Royal Belfast Academical Institution to teach Latin, Greek and Divinity. He later became Senior Housemaster and Head of the Divinity Department, remaining for over 30 years.

In 1973, Con was elected to represent Holywood, Cultra and Craigavad on the newly-created North Down Borough Council. He served as Deputy and then Mayor of North Down four times. One memorable visit to Bangor Castle was that of Prime Minister Margaret Thatcher who came with Christmas greetings on 22 December 1982.

Con became a founder member of the American Youth Foundation and for ten summers went to Camp Miniwanca on Lake Michigan, teaching sailing and lecturing. In 2010 Con was awarded a Millennium Fellowship by the UK Government to go to Kangaroo Island in Australia for research into the rapid decline of echidna.

In 1962, Con purchased an old water mill and farm yard at Port Braddan, in North Antrim. There he developed an old farm building into a small ecumenical family chapel for members and clergy of Catholic, Reformed and Orthodox churches. Over the years more than £100,000 was raised for local charities.

An eminent local historian, Con has made an immense contribution to Holywood through his books about the town's past. His first book was published in 2002 – *Holywood Then and Now.* His second was *Forgotten Houses of Holywood.* Next came *Letters to a Causeway Coast Mill House.* In 2006 he published *Rosamond Praeger, The Way That She Went.*

DR ROGER BLANEY

Dr Blaney graduated from Queen's University, Belfast as a medical doctor in 1957. After a number of hospital appointments, he with his wife, Brenda, returned from London to Northern Ireland and finally set up home in Croft Road, Holywood. Dr Blaney specialised in Public Health Medicine and was Head of that Department at Queen's University before he retired in 1988. In the same year he completed his seminal publication *Belfast – 100 years of Public Health* marking a hundred years of city status.

Dr Blaney learned Irish both at home and after school. He won a scholarship to study further in the Gaeltacht in Donegal. He has since written extensively on the history of the Irish language. In particular, he traces the Presbyterian Irish-speaking tradition from its early roots in Gaelic Scotland, through the Plantation and Williamite War periods to its successive revivals in the 18th, 19th and 20th centuries.

Covers of two of Roger Blaney's books

In his book *Presbyterians and the Irish Language* (1996) he contends that at a time when the Irish language was losing ground to a combination of forces, it was the Presbyterians who were to the fore in saving valuable Irish manuscripts, and in teaching and preaching through Irish. This history adds significantly to the mutual understanding between the main traditions of our island and provides evidence for the view that we share more than that which divides us.

In 1999, Dr Blaney published *Nótaí ón Lia*, a book on medical issues, in the Irish language. He has been a Fellow of the Ullans Academy since 2009, and is currently deputy chair.

During the past few decades, Dr Blaney has been very involved in the Holywood Branch of the Gaelic League (which was established in 1921). The aim of the Gaelic League is the non-political promotion of the Irish language to the community at large. The Branch organises the Nasca Community Festival in Holywood every March. It also provides Irish language evening classes.

There has been a tradition of Irish-speaking in Holywood. At the beginning of the 17th century, the great majority of the residents would have spoken it, and there was still a significant proportion in the 19th century. Nowadays 5% have some knowledge of the language.

The Blaney family home was once occupied by the sculptor Rosamond Praeger and her naturalist brother Robert Lloyd Praeger.

DR JOHN ST CLAIR BOYD

John St Clair (pronounced Sinclair) *Boyd* was an Irish gynaecologist and first President of the Belfast Gaelic League.

Boyd, a member of the Church of Ireland, was born in December 1858 at *Cultra House* in Holywood, His father, John Kane Boyd, the joint owner of the Blackstaff Mill in Belfast, is buried in Holywood.

John studied medicine at Queen's College, Belfast. After a short stint in Edinburgh (where he met his wife), he worked for a time in the Birmingham and Midland Hospital with Lawson Tait, a distinguished surgeon. Boyd returned in 1888 to Belfast to work at the Hospital for Sick Children, Queen Street, as assistant surgeon.

He became gynaecologist at the Ulster Hospital for Children and Women (then situated in Fisherwick Place). Boyd is renowned as having carried out the first hysterectomy in Northern Ireland in 1889 (which involved the use of a corkscrew). In 1894 he successfully delivered a baby by caesarean section – another pioneering operation in Belfast. Boyd was recorded as being very popular with his patients, with a caring attitude.

Politically, it is known that Boyd was a staunch – though liberal – Unionist. However he became a member of the Gaelic League, *Conradh na Gaeilge,* founded in Dublin in 1893. It is recorded that in the annual election to the League's governing body, he received nearly as many votes as Pádraig Pearse. When the Belfast Gaelic League was established just two years later, with its inaugural meeting in PT McGinley's home on the Beersbridge Road, Boyd was elected its first President, holding the post for many years. The League promoted the use of the Irish language; in one of his addresses to members of the League, Boyd stressed the need for it to ensure that *'such a beautiful and noble language should not die'.*

He also served as President of the Dublin Pipers' Club and adjudicated at music festivals. In 1893 he joined the Belfast Naturalists' Field Club, for which he read a paper on the Irish language and wrote a number of articles. With the Club he visited Tory Island and spent time in the Gaeltacht. He also built up a valuable art collection.

Boyd died on 10 July 1918, and is buried under a magnificent Celtic cross in Belfast City Cemetery.

JOE CAMPBELL

Joe Campbell was born on 20 July 1946 in the Kinnegar Nursing home. His father worked in a wholesale grocers in Belfast. The Kinnegar, bounded by the railway and the sea, was then much smaller than today. The Holywood Yacht club was the centre of adult and young people's social activity. Kinnegar Ordnance Depot provided work for several hundred – mostly men – with Army vehicles almost the only traffic disturbing the street football.

Joe first went to the church school on Church Road, then the new Holywood Primary School opened; he later attended Holywood Secondary School (now Priory College). Just before he was 15 he went to work as a message boy in Harland and Wolff, prior to an apprenticeship as an engineer at 16. He had day release from the shipyard as well as night classes in Bangor and Belfast Technical Colleges. Joe worked on the fitting out of several ships and went out on some while they were on trial.

His family were members of 1st Holywood Presbyterian Church (Bangor Road). Joe became a committed Christian at 20 years old, and this changed the direction of his life. After a year's course at the Belfast Technical College, he got a post in Ballygomartin Boys School at the top of the Shankill Road, teaching metalwork, craft and design. After a couple of years, he was asked to run the school outdoor centre called Ardaluin, just outside Newcastle. He lived on site and every week welcomed 25 boys and two teachers to enjoy camping, canoeing, sailing, gardening and – crucially – looking after themselves, including cooking and cleaning.

Four years later, Joe was asked by the City of Belfast YMCA to run a new youth facility in Wellington Place. It was then a club for teens and twenties boys and girls, six nights a week, with a couple of thousand members, four staff and a team of volunteers. It was cross-community, in a city tearing itself apart. After 11 years Joe moved to work on front-line peace-building with Mediation Northern Ireland. This involved working as a mediator in community disputes, often at Belfast's peace-lines, as well as among prisoners and paramilitaries, and with politicians, police and Army officers.

Joe ended his working life in Nepal, seconded by a Christian Mission agency supporting the Ministry of Peace and Reconstruction in Kathmandu for four years. Since then he has contributed to work in Afghanistan and South Sudan. In many tight spots over the years Joe has often thought '*what's a wee lad from the Kinnegar doing in a place like this*'?

SIR ROBERT COOPER

Sir Bob, as he was usually known, was born in 1936 in Castlefin, County Donegal. His mother was a schoolteacher, and his father owned the general store in the village. Bob was educated at Foyle College in Londonderry and then Queen's University in Belfast where he graduated in law in 1958, having been secretary – followed by chairman – of the Young Unionists.

In August 1970, as rioting spread in Northern Ireland, he was one of a group who sought to create a central political party designed to bring Protestants and Catholics together to work for a just society. He became the new Alliance Party's first general secretary and then deputy leader to Oliver Napier. They were involved in the Sunningdale talks in 1973 which led to the 1974 power-sharing Executive, in which Bob was the Minister for Manpower Services, and was in the forefront of trying to resist the Ulster Workers Council strike of that year.

Bob continued to represent West Belfast in successive Assemblies until 1976, when he was appointed first Chairman of the new Fair Employment Agency. This body was succeeded by the Fair Employment Commission which he continued to chair until 1999. As an arbiter of employment practices for 23 years, he was most influential in rooting out old discriminatory practices in Northern Ireland, though he had to endure relentless criticism from both sides of the community.

He was also a member of the Standing Advisory Commission on Human Rights which advised the Secretary of State on a wide range of human rights issues. His concern to create a better society coloured his entire life; for example he was a founder and Governor of Lagan College, the first integrated school in Northern Ireland where his children were educated.

For many years, the Coopers lived in Marino. Sir Bob died at his home in 2004, and is survived by his wife Pat and their two children, William and Anne.

Sir Bob and Lady Cooper

BERTHA RUSSELL GEDDES

Miss Bertha Geddes was a highly regarded stalwart among Holywood Presbyterians, an excellent teacher, local historian and an active member of the Irish language community. She was born in 1905 in Holywood, and reared in her parents' home at 7 Church Road which was then the town's Post Office (now Knott's Bakery). Her mother, Mary Dorothea née Russell, was the postmistress, the first woman in Ireland to hold such a post. Bertha's father was Robert Geddes, an insurance agent, and assistant with the postal services. Bertha's sisters were Victoria Margaret Gillespie and Dorothy Mary Tait, the latter a well-known journalist for the Holywood area.

Bertha went to the local parochial school and later Sullivan Upper. She regularly attended Sunday school, and was greatly influenced by the young teacher Jim Reid, who inspired her to take an interest in Irish culture. He gave her a copy of Eleanor Hull's classic book, on Cuchulain, which he signed for her in Irish. Bertha treasured this all her life. Bertha then joined the Gaelic Fellowship run by the YMCA where classes and social events through Irish were organised for Protestants by John Pasker.

Bertha was awarded a King's Scholarship and entered Stranmillis College, Belfast. She secured a teaching post in Percy Street Elementary School in the Shankill district of Belfast, retiring from there in 1965. In mid-career, she undertook the study of languages at Trinity College Dublin, graduating in 1947. By this time she was taking part in Gaelic activities in Holywood. She began teaching Irish under the auspices of the Holywood Irish Society of which she was secretary for many years. She took full part in the activities of the Irish-speaking community, regularly meeting in each other's houses. She visited the Donegal Gaeltacht and enjoyed talking to the people in their own dialect.

Other historical interests included research into her own family origins. She admired William Russell of Ballymagee, Bangor, a prominent leader of the 1798 Rebellion who, with his two brothers, took part in the Battle of Ballynahinch and later suffered execution. Another ancestor, Colonel Andrew Blakely of Hillsborough, fought as a Confederate in the American Civil War.

Bertha was a firm supporter of the Ulster Liberal Party. In 1981 she moved from her home in the Crescent to Bangor West. She died on 5 November 1997 and is buried in the Old Priory Graveyard in Holywood.

A copy of a talk she gave in 1977 on '*Holywood as I remember it*' is held in the Library archive.

JESSIE GETTY

Jessie in her VAD uniform

Jessica Getty (née Roberts) was born in March 1894. She was from a Protestant family background and she held strong unionist beliefs. In September 1912 she signed the Ulster Covenant against Irish Home Rule in Belfast City Hall.

But during the next couple of years as tensions grew high in the North of Ireland, the First World War erupted in Europe. In 1914 when a call was made for volunteers to nurse the wounded soldiers in Europe – Jessie joined in the war effort as a Voluntary Aid Detachment Nurse (VAD). She worked in Wimereux Base Hospital in Northern France – close to the battlefield.

One impressive tale in Jessie's life story is about her nursing a young soldier. She said it was late one evening when one of her patients gestured over to her. He had something to give her. It was his rosary beads which he handed over to her. This young man was dead before dawn. Jessie never forgot the young soldier and his rosary beads were one of her most treasured possessions until her death.

Jessie was awarded the Red Cross Medal 1914–18 for her service as a VAD during the First World War. She returned home and went to work in the military hospital in Belfast. She gained lodgings in Belfast in the same house as a young army officer who had served with the Royal Irish Rifles. He had been badly wounded by a shell and a fellow officer lifted a handful of 'glar' (mud) from the bottom of the trench and put it on his forehead to try to stop the bleeding. This probably saved his life and a short time later he was picked up by stretcher bearers and taken to hospital.

This young army officer became Jessie's husband and he trained to become a solicitor. He was employed in Belfast by Moorehead and Wood and later he worked for Holywood Urban Council until his death in 1976. Since sustaining his injuries in the First World War he occasionally had small pieces of shrapnel coming out of his body. He gave many of these pieces to Jessie who put them into matchboxes. When he died, Jessie buried the pieces of shrapnel with him!

Jessie lived a long and full life. She became Northern Ireland's 'most senior citizen' when she died just three months before her 108th birthday. She passed away in December 2001. Her photographs and wartime memorabilia are now proudly displayed in the Somme Heritage Museum just outside Newtownards.

WALDEMAR HEININGER

Waldemar Heininger was the son of Rudolf and Annabella (née Smith) and lived at *Byronville* in the Kinnegar area of Holywood. Rudolf Heininger had come from his native Germany to Northern Ireland to work as a lithographer and printer. He and Annabella married in Belfast in August 1883, and had eight children. (Previously they had lived at no. 1 High Street, just past Ean Hill.)

Waldemar, who was known outside the family as Walter, was born on 30 December 1896, and baptised in April in St Philip and St James parish church, Holywood – the seventh child of the marriage. It is known that he joined the newly-formed 1st Holywood Scout Troop.

Waldemar Heininger on the Holywood war memorial

When the First World War broke out, he volunteered to serve, in the 11th Battalion, Royal Irish Rifles. He was killed in action on the first day of the battle at the Somme on 1 July 1916, aged just 20. He is commemorated on the memorial plaque in the parish church, and on the war memorial in Redburn Square.

Although he was born and reared in Holywood, it might seem odd that he volunteered to fight against the country of his father, especially as it appears that his older brother Leopold, fought for the Germans in the same war. Heininger is worthy of note as '*the German who fought for Ulster*'. During the war, his mother changed her surname to Henning, to make it less Germanic.

After her husband Rudolf's premature death in 1899 aged just 42, Annabella took in laundry to supplement the family income – '*no machines used*' was her advertising slogan. It is known that in the 1920s, she had a contract for laundering table cloth from Harland and Wolff shipyard.

One of Waldemar's sisters, Miss Henning, continued to live in the Kinnegar until her death in 1993.

Waldemar, together with his brother Leopold, featured prominently in Holywood author and broadcaster Padraig Coyle's play *Silent Night* which was performed in the church of St Philip and St James in November 2016.

SIR ROBERT KENNEDY

Sir Robert Kennedy was born on 24 December 1851 at the newly-built Bangor Castle, the residence of his uncle RE Ward. He was the son of Robert Stuart Kennedy of Cultra House and Anne Catherine, the daughter of Edward Michael Ward of Bangor and Lady Matilda Stewart, the daughter of the 1st Marquess of Londonderry.

In 1874, after obtaining a degree at Oxford University, he entered the Spanish Department in the Foreign Office. His first served for three years in Madrid at a time of civil strife. From 1877 to 1879, he served in Constantinople with Sir Henry Layard, the British ambassador there. In 1880, when Lord Dufferin was appointed ambassador at St Petersburg in Russia, he chose Robert Kennedy as his private

Sir Robert and Lady Kennedy with Lady Baden Powell at the Cultra Manor scout hut

secretary. Both men were at a military review when a bomb went off, killing Tsar Alexander. In 1882, Robert was appointed chargé d'affaires in Sofia, Bulgaria.

In November that year, while on leave, he visited Castleward where he met and became engaged to the Honourable Bertha Jane Ward, daughter of the 5th Viscount Bangor, his cousin, marrying her the following year. Until 1884 he was chargé d'affaires in Romania, and then secretary of Legation to Persia until 1893 when he was appointed minister to Montenegro. In 1906, he became ambassador to Uruguay, a post he held until his retirement in 1912.

Robert Kennedy retired to *Cultra Manor* which he had had built in 1902. He was knighted in 1913. His wife, was said to be *'the perfect British Embassy wife, and the outstanding Ulster adventuress of the Edwardian age, and the first European woman to enter Khorasan and Afghanistan'*.

Sir Robert and Lady Kennedy both died in 1936, leaving their four daughters to inherit the estate. Two of them, Maud and Kathleen, had volunteered as nurses in the First World War, serving with distinction in Salonika.

In 1961, *Cultra Manor* was sold to the Ulster Folk Museum. After major reconstruction work, the Museum was initially opened to visitors in 1964. The Manor was further restored and reopened in 2011.

Kennedy was a friend of Lord Baden-Powell, and supported the establishment of the 1st Holywood Boy Scout Troop, known to this day as *'Sir Robert Kennedy's Own'*. Baden-Powell often stayed at *Cultra Manor*, visiting the troop at their den in the woods. Kennedy gave the troop their first colours, the Union flag bearing on its flagpole a dolphin (part of the Kennedy coat-of-arms). This was later given to the Northern Ireland Scout Association by whom it is now used as a trophy for water activities – the Kennedy Dolphin.

EILEEN KINGHAN AND NANA HOUSTON

Eileen Kinghan was born on 26 October 1908, the youngest child of Matilda and Samuel Kinghan. The family came to Holywood in the early 19th century and lived on High Street where they had a business as coal merchants and agents for the Glen Laundry.

Eileen was a member of High Street Presbyterian Church as well as being successful at music festivals. She taught singing to local children and went on to form and conduct Holywood Children's Choir which performed for many years around the Christmas tree in the town. In her working life, Eileen was secretary to the Town Clerk of Holywood Urban District Council, Bruce Stevens; her brother, Leonard, was the Holywood Council's Rate Collector.

Eileen with her brother Leonard and the Holywood scrapbook

Such was Eileen's love of her home town that she compiled a scrapbook of events in Holywood, mainly in the 1950s and 1960s, which became a popular reference book for residents throughout the years. This impressive scrapbook is now in our local Library and remains a source of information for the local University of the Third Age (U3A) Archive Group and visitors.

Eileen Kinghan died on 5 March 1986, aged 77, and is remembered for her foresight in keeping such an historic record of events in Holywood.

Annie (Nana) Preston Houston (née Ward) was born on 22 July 1921 at her grandparents' dairy farm, *Laburnum Cottage,* the Kinnegar, Holywood, the youngest daughter of Frank and Mary Ward. The family moved to Airdrie, Scotland and it was here that the eight year-old Nana won her first prize in elocution. Thus began her lifelong love of the spoken word and music.

Returning to Holywood to 3 Sullivan Place, Nana gained diplomas in both elocution and music.

She was a member of Belfast Cathedral choir under the leadership of Frank Capper and was a faithful member of High Street Presbyterian Church choir which benefited from her lovely contralto voice.

Nana taught elocution from her home at 114 Church Road with many local children gaining confidence in speech and drama through competing in Holywood Music Festival and further afield. She was closely involved in the organisation of this festival and acted as adjudicator in festivals throughout the country. She also taught in Sullivan Upper School, Belfast's Bloomfield Collegiate and Ashleigh House, and served on the Board of Governors of various schools in Holywood.

Nana married Cecil Houston and continued to live in Holywood.

She died on 7 December 2001 and is fondly remembered for her contribution to the town.

STEWART AND JEAN McCADDEN

Stewart McCadden, at the age of 21, started a Boy Scout Troop in Holywood, during the Second World War. This was named 3rd Holywood, as 1st and 2nd Holywood Scouts already existed.

Over the years, this Group carried on scouting activities in various venues over the town. In the Troop's early years, they obtained an old hall on Ean Hill

Stewart McCadden at the 70th reunion of the 3rd Holywood Scout Troop

which served them faithfully well into the 1960s. In addition to their camps all over the UK and abroad, they raised funds for a new hall. One of their events was an Annual Fete, held in Redburn House and its grounds. These efforts enabled them to create purpose-built accommodation on Ean Hill with many rooms and storage for canoes, tents, etc. They had a store outside where they kept the newspapers which they collected to raise funds. They continued a healthy Group with Venture Scouts, Rover Scouts, Scouts, Wolf Cubs (later Cub Scouts), and Beaver Scouts.

Stewart was a Scoutmaster of the old school, affectionately known as 'Skipper'. There are many of his boys around today who would testify to the principles which he instilled in them, following Lord Baden-Powell's standards of fairness and good healthy living.

In later life Stewart married Jean McArdle, who was an outstanding support to him, especially in publishing *KITBAG* (*Keep In Touch, Be A Giver*), the magazine still used to keep in touch with his Scouts across the world. He passed away in 2015. A plaque commemorating Stewart was placed in the High Street, in 2018.

Jean McCadden is well-known in the North Down area for teaching Scottish Country Dancing. This she has done for over 60 years. She has taken her girls to displays and competitions in Scotland and at home. Her Craighelen Dancers are a mixed group of adults who give many dancing displays. Over the years, Jean has taught four generations of at least two families and continues to teach Scottish Country Dancing to an enthusiastic mixed group in Helen's Bay.

Jean was also a school teacher, initially helping to run a private infant school in Helen's Bay for over twenty years and then teaching at the Warren private school. When that closed, she was asked to go to Rockport Preparatory School, from which she retired 18 years later.

In addition, she played the organ in Helen's Bay Presbyterian church for a number of years, and has now been playing the organ for 44 years in the Non-Subscribing Presbyterian church in Holywood, and on occasions in the garrison church at Palace Barracks.

THOMAS VALENTINE PLAISTED McCAMMON

Lieutenant Colonel Thomas Valentine Plaisted McCammon served in the Royal Irish Rifles (RIR). Born in 1874 in Holywood, he was the son of Colonel Thomas Andrew McCammon (5th Battalion RIR). He joined his father's Regiment shortly after his 17th birthday.

TVP McCammon served with the Royal Irish Rifles in the Boer War and was promoted to Major in 1902. The following year he married Charlotte Garratt from Helen's Bay in Glencraig parish church. He served on the Holywood Urban District Council, chairing it for a while, and was a member of the Ulster Unionist Council and a prominent Orangeman.

On 18 June 1904, McCammon's daughter Catherine was baptised at St Philip and St James; McCammon recorded his occupation in the register as *Gentleman*. He was also a member of Holywood Masonic Lodge No. 381 which met in the newly-built Masonic Hall in Sullivan Place which was dedicated in January 1905 to the memory of his father who had been a prominent Mason in County Down.

In January 1913 TVP McCammon took command of the 5th Battalion RIR, and acted for a time as Assistant Adjutant and Quartermaster-General of the Ulster Division. (McCammon had also commanded a detachment at the coronation of King George V.)

A Boer War poster

During the Great War, he was heavily involved in recruitment, and raised the 20th (Reserve) Battalion, while based at Palace Barracks.

Lieutenant Colonel McCammon applied to be sent to the front, and this request was granted in April 1917 when he was attached to a Battalion of the Hampshire Regiment. After a very short period in France, he died on 28 April that year as a result of a shell wound received at Monchy-le-Preux. When he was initially been reported as wounded, his wife and her brother travelled immediately from Holywood to France.

At its meeting on 30 April, Holywood Urban District Council recorded '*its extreme regret at the sad news of the death*'. Councillor Orr spoke of his '*sterling qualities both in civilian life and as a soldier, and his love of Holywood and all that pertained to its welfare*'.

McCammon has an individual memorial tablet in Holywood parish church, as well as in Down Cathedral, Downpatrick.

Lieutenant Colonel McCammon also featured prominently in Padraig Coyle's play *Silent Night*.

ROBERT McCARTNEY QC

Bob McCartney was born in 1936, the youngest of eight children in a house on the Shankill Road. After primary school and having passed the first Qualifying Test he attended Grosvenor High School and gained a scholarship to Queen's University. His brothers and sisters had moved away and his father had died, so when his mother went to Canada to live with her daughter, Bob at 17 was the only member of his family in Belfast. He survived his years at Queen's by working at weekends and in the holidays but mostly with the kind hospitality of his future parents-in-law.

He graduated in law in 1954 but could not afford to enter the legal profession. He taught in a secondary school for a year and then found a solicitor who paid him a small income to do his apprenticeship. Having qualified as a solicitor, he realised he really wanted to be a barrister and with the support of his wife Maureen he studied for Bar Finals and attained his ideal workplace in 1968. He was outstandingly successful as a defence barrister for the leading insurance companies and businesses and when he was appointed a Queen's Counsel (QC) in 1975, it was the shortest period from the beginning of his practice.

Bob was always interested in pro-Unionist politics and in 1981 was elected to the Assembly to represent North Down as an Ulster Unionist. He was able to continue his profession and attend Stormont. In 1985 he spoke out strongly against the Anglo-Irish Agreement arguing for equal citizenship in a totally integrated relationship within the UK. He argued then that a power sharing executive would eventually squeeze out the middle ground and lead to the rise of the two extreme parties. He was expelled from the Ulster Unionists and formed a new party – the UK Unionist Party.

In 1987 he stood against Jim Kilfedder for the Westminster North Down seat and greatly reduced his majority; when Kilfedder died in 1995 Bob won the seat as an independent and retired from the Bar. He lost his seat to Lady Hermon in 2001 but continued in the Assembly till 2007. During his time representing North Down he wrote many articles on the Northern Ireland situation but also championed causes such as fair collection of rates and particularly the maintenance of the Grammar school system which had given him such a good start in life.

Bob still lives in Cultra with his wife Maureen while his son and two daughters are in London and another daughter is in Australia.

TONY MERRICK

Tony Merrick has lived in and around Holywood nearly all his life – his family moved from Belfast in 1951. He started to take an interest in local history and the built environment in the 1960s, and combined this with his interest in photography. This led also to a study of family history, both local and personal.

Tony trained as an architectural technician, and between 1980 and his retirement in 2004, worked for the Hearth Housing Association which specialised in the restoration of old and listed buildings for social housing.

For many years Tony was a member of the Committee of the Holywood Residents Association. Since 2003, he has also served on the Committee of the Holywood Conservation Group; this body exists to encourage the preservation of what is best in both our built and natural environment, and also to promote architecture that is sensitive to the surroundings where new development takes place.

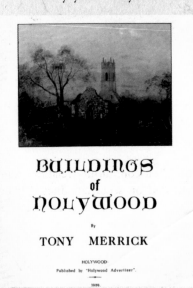

BUILDINGS
of
HOLYWOOD

By

TONY MERRICK

HOLYWOOD:
Published by "Holywood Advertiser".

1986.

The cover of Buildings of Holywood

Both these voluntary organisations, and the many Holywood residents who have taken a leading role in them, have played a significant part in the creation of Holywood town as it is today.

Tony has published a considerable number of articles and books. One which is of particular value to those interested in understanding the origins and development of the town of Holywood, (though sadly now out of print), is his *Buildings of Holywood*, published by the *Holywood Advertiser* in 1986.

Other publications include sections of the multi-volume series *Gravestone Inscriptions of Belfast,* and *Gravestone Inscriptions of County Down.* He has also written on the history of the parish of Holywood (up to 1900), the Parish Church of St George, High Street, Belfast, and 26 articles in *Irish Weekly,* entitled *Glimpses of Old Belfast.*

SIR OLIVER NAPIER

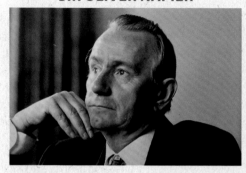

Sir Oliver Napier was a founder member and one time leader of the Alliance Party. He was also a well-known lawyer in a long-established family practice in Belfast.

Oliver Napier was born in Belfast on 11 July 1935 and educated at St Malachy's College in Belfast, (being the third generation of his family to attend the school).

He graduated in law from Queen's University. He became a successful solicitor, later practising in insolvency cases, but he became more widely-known as leader of the Alliance Party.

Alliance was established in 1970 at a time when community relations and politics in Northern Ireland were sharply divided on sectarian lines. Oliver Napier was a committed Roman Catholic, but he had a vision of an effective political party which could cross religious and political boundaries.

Given his passion, commitment and eloquence, he was a natural choice as co-leader (with Bob Cooper) of Alliance. In the power-sharing Northern Ireland Executive set up after the Sunningdale Agreement of December 1973, he was given a Ministerial appointment as Head of the Office of Law Reform. Despite the demise of the power-sharing Government in summer 1974, Oliver Napier and Alliance constantly worked to develop and consolidate a political middle-ground.

Napier was a shrewd politician and a good campaigner, and in the 1979 General Election he narrowly failed to win Protestant East Belfast with 15,066 votes, (polling only 928 votes fewer than the DUP's Peter Robinson and 864 fewer than the Ulster Unionist Bill Craig).

When he stepped down as Alliance leader in 1984 the then Secretary of State Douglas Hurd said that everyone who had sought a political solution to the complexities of Northern Ireland owed Oliver Napier a deep debt of gratitude. In 1985 he was knighted for his services to politics. During his career he was also a Belfast City Councillor, and from 1988 to 1992 he was chairman of the Standing Advisory Committee on Human Rights.

Oliver and his wife Briege moved to Holywood in the 1970s. They had nine children. Oliver died in 2011. His funeral service took place in St Colmcille's church and he is buried in Redburn cemetery.

DENNIS WILLIAM OGBORN

Dennis Ogborn was born on 24 June 1926. That year his father bought a bungalow next to Holywood Methodist Church. Dennis' parents were from Birmingham and his father had served with the Somerset Light Infantry Regiment, coming to Palace Barracks in 1918.

Dennis attended the Parochial School in Church Road. Unfortunately before he could finish his education, he needed a job to help the family financially. He started at just 15 as an apprentice fitter in Harland and Wolff. Records state he was 'a young man of the highest principles, outstanding integrity and utterly reliable'.

In January 1945, Dennis was travelling on one of the trains involved in the tragic Ballymacarrett accident. Completing his apprenticeship in 1946, Dennis remained in the shipyard for three years as a draughtsman until he decided that he wanted to be a teacher. After further studies, Dennis taught in various establishments including the Colleges of Technology in Banbridge, Bangor and Belfast. The pinnacle of his career was his appointment as Principal Lecturer in Educational Studies at the Ulster Polytechnic, Jordanstown.

Dennis was always wanting to improve Holywood. He was honorary secretary of the Holywood Residents Association, he organised the annual Keep Holywood Tidy campaign and was instrumental in Holywood winning the Best Kept Town award on several occasions. In May 2014, the Residents Association presented him with a commemorative seat which was placed in front of the Library.

He also helped establish the Citizens Advice Bureau, the Hob Youth Club and the Holywood Probus Club. He was an active member of the Holywood Road Safety Committee, Holywood Community Council, and a member of the Board of Governors of Redburn and St Patrick's Primary Schools, and Holywood Nursery School.

After many approaches from residents, Dennis agreed to stand for the North Down Council and in 1989 was elected to serve Holywood. In the 1993 elections, he 'topped the poll'. He maintained he could serve all the people better as an Independent Council member, and in 2001 was made an Alderman. In the Queen's Birthday Honours list in 1996 he was awarded the MBE for services to the community.

Dennis, a committed Christian since his late teens, has been a faithful member of Holywood Methodist Church for seventy years, welcoming visitors and calling on members of the congregation. Dennis believed 'if Christians everywhere were known for their neighbourliness, what an impact it would have on those outside the church'.

Dennis Ogborn did much to make Holywood what it is today.

HENRY HARRISON AND SARAH CECILIA HARRISON

The Harrison family were a very important part of Holywood's development from the 1850s until the sale of their estate which included much of the town in 1917. The first John Harrison was a ship-owner then living at *Mertoun Hall* who purchased *Holywood House*. He had two sons – the younger, Henry, lived at *Holywood House* with his wife Letitia, a niece of Henry Joy McCracken. (The older son, Captain John, lived on at *Mertoun*.)

Henry's son – another Henry – was born in Holywood in 1867. While a student at Oxford University, **Henry Harrison** became secretary of the Oxford Union Home Rule Group. Aged just 22, he was elected Nationalist Member of Parliament for mid-Tipperary in 1890, though in his support of Charles Stewart Parnell, the famous Irish nationalist, he lost his seat two years later.

Henry as a journalist, *courtesy of the Collection: Dublin City Gallery The Hugh Lane*

After Parnell's premature death in 1891, Harrison accompanied the body back to Dublin and supported Katharine O'Shea in Brighton.

Aged 47, he volunteered to serve in the First World War, joining the Royal Irish Rifles. Captain Harrison won the Military Cross for bravery on two occasions. (He and his American wife lost their only son who also volunteered, as a result of injuries he received fighting at Gallipoli.) Later Harrison worked as a journalist and author, writing many books, pamphlets and letters on Irish politics, including in 1931 *Parnell Vindicated*. Between the wars, he campaigned for Dominion status for Ireland within the British Empire.

His uncle, Captain John Harrison of *Mertoun Hall*, was a staunch Unionist, so they were at opposite ends of the political spectrum. (It was he who owned much of Holywood until 1917.)

Henry Harrison was buried in 1954 in the Old Priory Church, alongside other members of his family. The Parnell Society has arranged an annual commemorative service in Holywood in February in recent years.

Self-portrait by Sarah Cecilia Harrison, *courtesy of the Collection: Dublin City Gallery The Hugh Lane*

Harrison's sister, **Sarah Cecilia**, was born in Holywood in 1863. She trained as an artist at the Slade School of Fine Art, before moving to Dublin in 1889. She established herself as one of Ireland's foremost portrait artists. She also became the first woman to be elected to serve as a Dublin City Councillor in 1912.

She was also closely involved in Hugh Lane's efforts to establish an art gallery in Dublin, painting him in 1914, the year before he drowned when the *Lusitania* was torpedoed. Her portrait of Robert Lloyd Praeger hangs in the Ulster Museum. She died in 1941.

THE BRYSON FAMILY

Several generations of the **Bryson** family have been associated with Holywood. The first recorded were – the surprisingly long-lived – John (c.1685-1788) and Ann (c.1698-1804) Brison who were members of 1st Holywood Presbyterian Church, now the Non-Subscribing Congregation.

Their son James (c.1730-1796) became a Presbyterian minister in Banbridge, Lisburn and in the 2nd Belfast Congregation in Rosemary Lane. In 1791 he formed a new Church in Donegall Street (4th Congregation). James used his reputation to raise funds for the Belfast Poorhouse. As an active campaigner for Parliamentary reform and the emancipation of Presbyterians and Catholics, he became Chaplain to the 1st Belfast Company of Volunteers. He frequently dined in Belfast with Wolfe Tone, Napper Tandy and Thomas Russell.

James' first wife, Jane Stitt (died 1790) bore him at least 21 children but only three are known to have survived into adulthood. Jane and Mary, daughters of his second wife, became dressmakers in Belfast.

The surviving three sons were Andrew, Henry and Samuel. Andrew (1763-1797) became a Presbyterian minister in Dundalk. He preached in Irish to his own and other congregations nearby. Andrew had already gained a reputation *'as a person versed in the language and antiquities of the nation'* when he was invited to attend the Belfast Harp Festival on 11-13 July 1792 to record the words of the tunes played by the Irish Harpers.

Sadly Andrew did not attend due to failing health and died in March 1797. His wife, Ann McGlathery, died in 1802 after the family had moved to Rosemary Lane, becoming neighbours of the McCracken family into whom a younger sister married.

Henry Bell (c.1772-1829) was a schoolteacher in Cotton Court, Belfast. Samuel (1776-1853) studied surgery in Edinburgh, qualified as an apothecary in Dublin, married in 1805 and practised at 98 High Street, Belfast with two of his sons, Joseph Wallace and Samuel, both doctors. Early in life Samuel began to collect and transcribe Gaelic manuscripts containing histories, poems, songs and sermons, some belonging to his brother Andrew.

The Bryson family's houses on Holywood's Shore Road

Samuel's son, Joseph Wallace (1807-1855), continued living in one of the four Bryson properties in Shore Street, Holywood which were built in early 1833 and sold after Joseph's widow Olivia remarried in 1866. Joseph's eldest son Samuel (1847-1906), a linen merchant, lived in *Woodbank* on the Croft Road until his death and is buried in the Bryson family plot in Holywood Old Graveyard.

Bryson Street and Cluan Place in Ballymacarrett are named after Samuel Bryson's family home *Cluan* (Irish *cluain*, meadow).

DAVID HEWITT

David Hewitt was born in Belfast six days after the Second World War was declared. There has been a strong rugby tradition in his family, as his father, three uncles and two cousins were 'capped' for Ireland.

He played for Ulster as a schoolboy and he captained the Royal Belfast Academical Institution's Rugby Team to win the Schools Cup in 1957 (over Methodist College). Then he was 'capped' for Ireland in 1958, going on tour with the British Lions to Australia and New Zealand in 1959 (on which he was the top Lions points scorer in the Tests) and to South Africa in 1962.

Alongside his rugby achievements, he graduated in law from Queen's University, Belfast and soon became a partner in his father's law firm. He married Margaret Meharg in 1967 and moved to Holywood. They have four children and twelve grandchildren.

David has been an active leader in the Holywood community, as he established the Holywood Boys Crusader Class to teach the Bible in a creative and relevant way to young people who did not attend church. He has also promoted the interests and educational needs of young people by serving as a governor of Sullivan Upper School.

From 1994-97 he was the Independent Commissioner appointed to deal with complaints against the British Army. Following this, he was a member of the Northern Ireland Parades Commission for a number of years. He has also served as an elder in 1st Holywood Presbyterian

In action at a Lions match in New Zealand in 1959

Church for many years and in 1997 he was awarded a CBE for services to the community.

David is also a keen amateur artist and enjoys reading, classical music and holidaying in their family caravan in Donegal.

DAVID JEFFREY

David Jeffrey was born in Adair House, Ards Hospital, on 28 October 1962. David's childhood was spent in Dundonald where he lived with his parents and three younger siblings. He attended Christ Church Presbyterian, and was a pupil of Dundonald Primary School. His secondary education was at Dundonald Boys' High School and Sullivan Upper School, Holywood.

His mother's family lived in the Ballykeel Hills and his father is from Holywood. David's family returned to live in Holywood in 1981.

David had only one interest as a boy and that was to emulate George Best and play for his beloved Manchester United football team. David was scouted for Manchester United as a schoolboy. He enjoyed an apprenticeship and being a professional with the team for three years, David was the only team member who had studied latin!

In the summer of 1982, David joined Linfield where he played for ten years and was Club Captain for much of that time. In the 1984/85 European Cup he scored the crucial 'away goal' against Shamrock Rovers. David joined Ards FC in 1992 where he was player/coach, and then in February 1995, he joined Larne as a player/Assistant Manager.

In 1996 he returned to Linfield as Assistant Manager and in January 1997 he was appointed Manager, after Trevor Anderson. Alongside Roy Coyle, David Jeffrey is the most successful Manager in Linfield's history – both having won 31 trophies for the Club. During his time at Linfield, the Club won six League and Cup doubles in seven seasons, including winning the inaugural All-Ireland Setanta Cup in 2005. David was Linfield's longest serving Manager – 17 years and five months.

In 2014 Jeffrey stepped down as Linfield Manager. However in March 2016 he was appointed the new Manager of Ballymena United, guiding them to winning the Northern Irish League Cup in 2016/17, to the quarter-finals of the Tennants Irish Cup, to 4th place in the League, and European qualification.

Outside the football world, David has a successful career in Social Work, and currently practises as a Senior Social Worker in Larne Community Integrated Team.

David is also an enthusiastic member of the Ballykeel Conservative Flute Band and is the proud father of two adult sons.

RORY McILROY

Rory McIlroy was born in Holywood on 4 May 1989, the only child of Gerry and Rosie McIlroy. Gerry introduced Rory to golf very young, and his skill was immediately apparent: McIlroy reportedly hit a 40-yard drive at the age of 4, and made his first hole in one aged 9. Supported in his golf education by his parents, he left Sullivan Upper School at 16 to focus on the game.

Under the guidance of Holywood Golf Club's then professional, Michael Bannon, McIlroy began competing when he was a child. His first notable international win, at the age of nine, came in the Under 10 World Championship in Doral, Florida.

In 2005, McIlroy's score of 61 set a record at the North of Ireland Amateur Open at Royal Portrush. At 16, he became youngest player to win

Rory with the famous Claret Jug, after winning the Open in 2014

the West of Ireland Championship and the Irish Close Championship. He then took the 2006 European Amateur title, followed by a Silver Medal for the lowest amateur score at the Open Championship in 2007. Later the same year, aged 18, Rory reached the top of the World Amateur Rankings and made a Walker Cup appearance at Royal County Down.

Rory then embraced the professional circuit, becoming the youngest golfer to secure his European Tour card. Rory claimed his first European Tour title in the Dubai Desert Classic early in 2009, and a PGA Tour victory followed at Quail Hollow in April 2010.

Rory had a check with reality at the 2011 Masters Tournament. With what had seemed likely to be a certain win at the beginning of the final day of the tournament, Rory let a commanding lead slip. But showing little or no scar tissue from Augusta's hard-learned lesson, Rory claimed his first Major at the US Open two months later at Congressional Country Club in Maryland. His 16-under total, with an eight-shot victory, was the lowest total score at a US Open.

A second Major win followed in 2012 with a further two secured in 2014. Rory joined the illustrious company of Jack Nicklaus and Tiger Woods as the only three golfers to have won four Major titles by the age of 25. He was ranked number 1 in the world for 95 weeks, initially achieving it in 2012. He has been an inspirational team player in several European Ryder Cup wins.

In January 2013 he set up (and subsequently endowed) the Rory Foundation, based in Holywood, to support children's charities around the world. In April 2017, Rory married Erica Stoll.

GEORGINA McKEOWN

Georgina (usually known as Ena) **McKeown** has a very proud position in Irish cycling history. For many years she has held the record for the fastest ride from Londonderry to Belfast, and the Mercian bicycle on which she achieved this feat is on display in the lower Transport Gallery at the Ulster Folk and Transport Museum.

Born in Sydenham, in 1917, she started cycling in her teens and quickly showed a natural talent. But she also trained hard, riding long distances several days a week, up to nearly 100 miles on a Saturday. She joined the Maryland Wheelers Club, Lisburn. Her first successes in competitions were on the track, but she soon turned to road racing.

The most important record that she broke was in a race from Londonderry to Belfast in 1953. She even had a puncture on the Glenshane Pass, and had to change bikes, and then a torn muscle in Toome. Her time was three hours and 46 minutes – 14 minutes less than the previous best. She also broke the record for ten miles, on the Moira Road.

Ena raced all over Ireland, and toured parts of the Continent on a bicycle, with her husband, Billy, himself a proficient cyclist. She recalls that they saw

Ena with some of her cups

the Tour de France on their honeymoon. She also attended the Casino at Monte Carlo in her cycling shorts!

The bicycle on which she rode from Londonderry to Belfast

In all, Ena won more than 90 prizes, including the Butler Cup outright, but sadly many of her trophies were destroyed during the German air raids in the Second World War. During the War, she and her mother had to move to a small cottage at Ballysallagh. Ena worked in one of the now-forgotten ammunition factories at Ballyrobert, helping to make cases for bullets and shells. (One of her sisters married an American soldier, and went to live there.)

Ena was also travelling on one of the two BCDR trains involved in the tragic accident at Ballymacarrett in January 1945. She was taken to hospital to be checked over, but fortunately was not seriously injured.

Ena moved to Holywood in what might be termed her 'retirement', although in practice she continued to be very fit, keeping on with the bicycling for many years. In 2017 she celebrated her 100th birthday. This year, she said '*I do miss it – I just lived on that bike. I had a great time cycling*'.

MARK POLLOCK

Mark Pollock is an inspirational person who has achieved much, notwithstanding severe disabilities.

He is the son of Johnny Pollock and Barbara Carson, born in 1976, growing up on Church Avenue in Holywood. He lost sight in his right eye when aged just five. He went to school at the Royal Belfast Academical Institution in Belfast, then when studying business and economics at Trinity College, Dublin, where he was a keen rower, he became totally blind. He was unable to take up a job offer in London, but returned to rowing and won silver and bronze medals for Northern Ireland in the 2002 Commonwealth Rowing Championships.

Mark also took up endurance sports, completing six marathons across the Gobi desert in seven days with a sighted partner, raising money for the charity *Sightsavers International*. In 2004, he competed in the North Pole marathon and went on to compete in the Dead Sea Ultra, Everest Marathon and Ironman Zurich. In 2008, with two sighted companions, he raced to the South Pole in the inaugural South Pole Race with six other teams. They travelled over 1,000 kilometres, hauling heavy sledges behind them, for 43 days. He was the first blind man to achieve this feat, narrowly finishing fifth in the race to the Pole.

By his early thirties, Mark had set up his own motivational speaking business (www.markpollock.com), and written a successful book *Making It Happen,* which described his struggle with blindness and his attempts to rebuild his life. Then in July 2010, he suffered a tragic fall from a second storey window, shortly before his wedding, breaking his back and fracturing his skull. He is now a wheelchair user.

However Mark has been challenging expectations, exploring the boundaries of spinal cord injury recovery. He is collaborating with scientists and technologists in America and elsewhere overseas, on experimental research to try to overcome his own paralysis and to help others in similar positions. He is the co-founder of a global running series, *Run in the Dark (www.runinthedark.org)*, which takes place in November each year, raising funds for the Mark Pollock Trust (www.markpollocktrust.org) which aims to cure paralysis.

Mark has been awarded an honorary doctorate by Queen's University, Belfast and another by the Royal College of Surgeons in Ireland. He was named as a *Young Global Leader* at the World Economic Forum, and is on the Board of the Christopher and Dana Reeve Foundation (USA). He is the subject of an acclaimed documentary called *Unbreakable,* and is a TED Global speaker and inspirational speaker at corporate events.

TREVOR RINGLAND

Trevor Ringland was born in Belfast in November 1959, and first lived in Finaghy Road North, West Belfast as part of a police family, moving on to Black's Road, where he attended Suffolk Primary School. His father served as a Police Officer in West Belfast at the time and was then promoted and transferred as a Sergeant to Glenarm, where the family lived in the police station. In those days the police were very much part of the community and Trevor is still known by some as the Sergeant's son.

It was during that time the Troubles broke out. His father was again transferred, moving to Larne. It was at Larne Grammar School that Trevor first came across rugby and started to play. In his penultimate year the small school made it through to the quarter finals of the Schools Cup. In those days Trevor used to play for the school in the morning and for one of the local club teams in the afternoon.

After school he went to Queen's University Belfast to study law and his rugby career developed there. He was part of a very successful Queen's rugby period, under the influence of various coaches including the late Jimmy Davidson, who professionalised their approach to fitness and how they played the game. The team won the League and Cup and Trevor was picked to play for the Irish and British Universities, then the Ulster team, and in 1981 the Irish team for his debut match against the touring Australian side.

Trevor was fortunate in his rugby career as Ireland won the Triple Crown in 1982 and 1985, and the Championship in 1983; he was selected to play for the British and Irish Lions on a tour to New Zealand in 1983, and against the Rest of the World team as part of the centenary celebrations of the International Rugby Board in 1986.

Throughout his rugby career it was the ethos of the sport that attracted Trevor – one of friendship and even during the worst of the Troubles, rugby managed to rise above the issues on the streets and show that friendship was a more constructive way of conducting relationships on this island.

Trevor now works as a lawyer. He is involved in various organisations including Peace Players International (which uses sport to build relationships), Co-operation Ireland and the *One Small Step* campaign which promotes a constructively shared future in Northern Ireland. He was a Trustee of the RUC GC Foundation for its first ten years. He lives in Holywood.